Best Wishes

J S Arnenas

Ball of Fire

An Autobiography

Fred Trueman

Ball of Fire

An Autobiography

J M Dent & Sons Ltd   London

First published 1976
© Fred Trueman, 1976

Made in Great Britain
at the Aldine Press, Letchworth, Herts
for J. M. Dent & Sons Ltd
Aldine House, Albemarle Street, London

This book is set in 12 on 14pt Monotype Baskerville 169

ISBN 0 460 04304 8

Contents

List of Illustrations

Acknowledgments

The author and publisher are grateful to the following for permission to reproduce photographs:

The South Yorkshire News Service (no. 1); D. C. Thomson & Co. Ltd, Manchester (no. 3); The National Coal Board (no. 4), Thames Television (no. 5); Sport & General (nos 7, 9, 11, 12, 14, 15, 16); Syndication International (nos 8, 10, 23); The *Yorkshire Post* (no. 18); Mirrorpic (no. 17); Dennis Dobson, Scarborough Photo/News Agency (nos 20, 21); *Derby Evening Telegraph* (nos 24, 26); Yorkshire Television (no. 28); The *Sunday People* (no. 29—photo by Harold Holborn); *The Times* (no. 30).

The author and publisher would also like to thank the Committee of the Northern Cricket Society and the Executors of the late Mr Royman Browne for permission to reproduce the line illustration on page 161.

Author's Note

There are few people I wish to thank, apart from those already mentioned in the text of this book—except Veronica for rescuing me, and Barry Cockcroft for help and advice.

It is eight years since I bowled my last delivery in competitive cricket for the County of the White Rose. They have now given me the honour of life-membership which is something I will always be proud of, being a member of what I consider to be still the greatest cricket club in the world.

Dedication

I dedicate this book to all young cricketers of independent spirit, in the hope that they might learn from it some of the pitfalls into which their pride and self-respect will surely lead them.

Chapter 1

Country Boy

It was snowing heavens high in south Yorkshire on the night of 6 February 1931 when my father ran out of the house to fetch the doctor. But I was too fast even then for most people. It was the usual run up, you know—a rhythmical approach and straight through. By the time the doctor arrived I was already born, all 14 lb. 1 oz. of me. My Grandmother Stimpson, whose maiden name was Sewards, had delivered me, which put her in a strong position when they decided what to call me. So, I was launched into the world as Frederick Sewards Trueman.

The world was a pretty bleak place in those days too, because by the time I was old enough to sit up and take notice there were six children in the Trueman family, and another one came thirteen years after that first, quick delivery of mine. On Dad's wage of around thirty-seven shillings from the pit there was nothing lavish about life at No. 5 Scotch Springs, Stainton, one of a terraced row of twelve houses owned by the colliery. The house is no longer there—it was demolished.

One of the myths about me says I come from an archetypal Yorkshire mining family. Now I'll admit my father was a coalface worker at Maltby Main and that I put in a few months myself at the same pit, but the Truemans were far from being a mining family in the same way as the others living around the same area who had known nothing but the pit for generations. We were basically country folk, reared from way back to handling horses. I believe we stemmed from the Bawtry area and my grandad Albert Trueman was a well-known horse dealer. During the First World War he travelled all over the country buying horses for the government so that they could be shipped out to the front in France. He must have been pretty good at cricket too, because he was invited to the Yorkshire nets in the 1880s and offered terms. But when he found out how much he could expect to earn as a Yorkshire cricketer in those days he told them where to go, adding that he earned more in one day sellings horses than they were offering for a week.

My father, Alan Thomas Trueman, was also brought up to horses, serving his time at Earl Fitzwilliam's stables at Wentworth Woodhouse to become a steeplechase and point-to-point jockey. But he became too heavy and had to go and work at Captain Adcock's place at Stainley Woodhouse. He knew horses all right, did my father. One of his tasks was to go all over the place with a travelling stallion, and anyone who knows anything about horse flesh will tell you that handling a rampant stallion being walked around the countryside to serve mares in season, by appointment, was one of the toughest jobs you could get. We used to have a great big photograph of that animal on the wall at home. He was a really beautiful horse, called Baby—of all things.

I don't suppose Dad much liked becoming a miner, but when he was a young man you were grateful to get any job at all. At least he found a house in Stainton, which was not, as many people try to make out, a mining village at all. It was very much in the country, surrounded by agricultural land. I grew up among fields and hedgerows and you wouldn't have known there was a colliery anywhere near, because it was more than a mile away and behind a hill. Dad used to walk there and back every day. We were lucky he was brought up the way he was because his knowledge of country ways meant that we never went hungry at a time when many people in large families like ours definitely did. He took over first one, then two and eventually four allotments, growing every kind of vegetable you can think of and rearing pigs and hens. We used to kill a pig twice a year so we generally had a nice piece of ham in the house. All we children had to help with the feeding and cleaning, boiling up the potato peelings and other scraps from the table to feed the pigs. Nothing was wasted in the Trueman household.

He was a hard man, was my Dad. Only about 5 ft. 6 in. in height but very broad and strong, he was a real stickler for discipline, a teetotaller and a God-fearing man. Three times every Sunday we went to Stainton parish church and there was no speaking out of turn in our house. Even when I was in my thirties I never dared answer my father back, and if any of us gave any lip to Mother we would get a belt round the ear. And if you didn't eat up your crusts at tea time they would be there on your plate at breakfast next day, and at lunch and tea until you ate them. My father had to work all hours to keep a good table and a warm fire for all nine of us, but I mainly remember feeling very sorry even as a kid for my mother, because she never stopped working day and night to keep things running smoothly. Just for a start, she had to bake eight or nine loaves every day. But she was always a very placid lady, and never said much.

Every now and again we used to eat very posh because Captain Adcock occasionally allowed Dad to shoot over his land, and he would come back with pheasant, partridge and rabbits. I got to know how to handle horses myself as a lad because my father would pick up a bit of extra money doing odd jobs and exercising the horses for the Captain. He took me with him and I would do things like muck out the stables and help to walk ten or twelve cattle to Doncaster market eleven miles away. I might get two bob from the Captain for that, which was a lot of money in 1938. In those days you would scrap for a penny. I learned how to ride too, and later on used to be allowed to exercise a big black hunter called Galengale, more than seventeen hands of a beast which would jump anything.

More extra money could be had at harvest time in Stainton, and all our family went into the fields picking peas for two shillings a hundredweight bag, digging out potatoes on cold and frosty mornings, topping and tailing turnips, weeding and hoeing. I earned another half a crown a week delivering newspapers and all the money went into the family coffers. But there still wasn't enough to spare for luxuries like holidays, and we got to the seaside for a day once a year on the Sunday school trip to Cleethorpes.

Hard they may have been, but I have very warm memories of those days because there was much love to go around the Trueman family and we were all very close. When there was no work to be done we would all go for long walks together in the countryside, gathering mushrooms, picking blackberries and finding hazel nuts. We had simple needs and pleasures. In fact, one of the greatest thrills of my young life was to walk down to the bottom of the lane and take down car numbers. To see a car round our village in the thirties was something of an event. An aeroplane was even more exciting, and I still remember vividly one evening when the whole village—

all 250 of us—turned out in the middle of a thunderstorm to watch a Royal Dutch airliner, a two-winged contraption, circling low over the houses and fields. We could see all the cabin lights and it seemed to be in trouble and looking for somewhere to put down. Eventually it flew away and next day we scoured the newspapers to see if there were any reports of an air crash but, thankfully, there were none.

Apart from the newspapers, we didn't have much communication with the outside world except for a crystal set and headphones, until one day Dad put an aerial up at the bottom of the garden and we could plug in a proper radio. At least our row had electricity put in by the colliery—the rest of the village still ran on gas. They weren't bad houses at all, really. We were a bit crowded with all us kids, but each of us had a bed to ourselves. The girls slept in one bedroom and the boys in another. Of course, the tranquillity of life was shattered in 1939 when the war started. I recall being frightened to death and wondering what the devil was going on as the German bombers came over looking for Sheffield. I stood there and watched from our village one Thursday evening as they hammered Sheffield out of sight. Guns were thumping away, the sky was full of flashes and flares and parachutes with landmines. But the biggest scare of my early life came later on in the forties when the air raid sirens sounded and a bit later we saw seven things like rockets with red lights droning through the sky. They called them doodle-bugs and they terrified me because you had to listen and wait for their engines to stop. If they kept going you were all right, but if they stopped you had to flatten yourself on the floor and hope. It meant they were coming down.

But the Germans weren't aiming for Scotch Springs, and the war for us was largely fought on the horizon and in the newspapers. Miners and a lot of the agricultural workers weren't called up because they were in essential work. The only real danger to my young life came once when I caught something dreadful called black measles when I was about three. I understand from my mother that it was a bit touch and go for a while. And then I nearly hanged myself at the age of seven whilst pinching apples. I was half way up the tree when I slipped and a branch went through the back of my shirt, jerking the collar against my windpipe. I passed clean out as I dangled there—it was the nearest thing to a public hanging Stainton had seen since the middle ages! Anyway, my pals pulled me down and I woke up in the arms of my mother. Apparently I began to tell her that I'd been talking to Jesus, so it must have been a close thing.

By and large, however, I did my best to stay out of trouble both at home and school, but I do admit that I became the extrovert of the family and always had plenty to say. I seem to remember being blamed for other people's sins even then, and getting into more bother because I had the nerve to stand up for myself. I can't help being like that—it's in my nature—but I had no idea in those days just what trouble it would create later on in life. When I started to go to the village school in Stainton I managed to steer clear of most problems. If the playground bullies tried to have a go at me in front of the others, for instance, I would bide my time until I got them on their own. They would never bother me again. I got on well with Miss Nelson and Miss Robinson, read everything I could get my hands on and was well ahead of most of the others in arithmetic. The school had only one room with a thin partition across it to divide the juniors from the seniors. I clearly remember one day hearing Miss Nelson through the partition, telling off the seniors because the cricket team had played very badly in one match and advising them to go and watch Freddie Trueman play cricket if they wanted to know what determination was all about. I was eight at the time and already showing some talent for the game, it seems. Cricket was very much part of the way of life in any Yorkshire village then and my father was completely devoted to the game, playing for Stainton every Saturday and taking me everywhere with him. He was the captain and a very good left arm spin bowler and batsman. I'd been bowling since the age of four, knocking over dustbin lids in our street, and by the time I was eight could bowl out men on the village green.

But to be truthful, I only played so much because of my father. I really wasn't so enthusiastic about the game as a lad but I didn't dare say so to him. Most of the other lads were dreaming about playing cricket for Yorkshire, but not me. Cricket was the only sport in the world as far as Dad was concerned, but I just tagged along. One thing, though—I always bowled fast, right from the start. It just happened naturally.

When I was twelve Dad decided to move house three and a half miles to Tennyson Road, Maltby. It was a bigger place and much nearer the shops for Mother, but I was unhappy to leave the countryside for a mining town. I started going to Maltby Secondary School having had to forget about my chances of going to grammar school. I reckon I was bright enough to pass the exam, but we just couldn't afford the school uniform, books and all the rest. Anyway, two schoolmasters called Dickie Harrison and Tommy Stubbs at the new school had the same sort of enthusiasm for cricket as my father. They watched me bowl and put me into the school team straight away, playing with and against lads quite a bit older than me. There was some resentment among a few of the seniors who were upset when a kid like me made the team and they gave me a bit of stick. They started to call me 'big head'. I'd never heard that expression before and didn't even know what it meant at first. But I got plenty of encouragement from Dickie Harrison. He used to practise regularly with the lads, and gave us some incentive by placing a penny on each off stump and a two bob piece on the middle. Then he invited us to bowl at him. Anything you knocked off you kept. I made a bob or two in a few weeks.

I was still only twelve and playing for Maltby School when I suffered the worst injury of my entire cricket career. Not only did it stop me playing for nearly two years, it almost took away my manhood. I was batting against a fast bowler at the time, and in those days didn't know there were such things as boxes or protectors for the genitals. And the ball caught me full in the groin.

They whipped me into hospital in Sheffield and for a long time the doctors thought there would be disastrous consequences. A big lump formed in my groin and for two years I limped around on a little cane stick. All that time I never laid hands on bat or ball—I couldn't. The same thing nearly happened ten years later playing at Northampton when Frank Tyson took the new ball and hit me with a full toss going at a fair lick. I was wearing a plastic protector then, but the ball smashed that into slivers and pushed them into my body. It hurt like hell and I thought to myself that I'd finish up a eunuch if I was going to get clobbered like this on a regular basis. My private parts shone like a rainbow for a full fortnight

—red, brown, blue, green and yellow they were. That injury was nowhere near as serious as the earlier damage; but there was no thought of giving up the game, and by the time I was fourteen I was back at the crease, bigger and stronger and bowling faster and faster.

At this stage Dad thought I ought to play proper club cricket, so he applied to Maltby Cricket Club to get playing membership for me. But they turned me down, saying they already had plenty of my sort. A small village club called Roche Abbey just outside Maltby did accept me, however, and I often have a quiet laugh about what happened next. Roche Abbey were drawn against Maltby in a knock-out competition. I took six wickets for about nine runs and we murdered them. The Maltby club was run from the pit where my father worked and they never left him alone after that. Their officials would follow Dad around his allotments offering him perks, even a better job at the pit if he would agree to letting me play for them. He even got a note from the colliery manager—left on his Davy lamp—but he told them all to get lost. He was a very proud man, my Dad.

I carried on playing for Roche Abbey and began to collect a lot of wickets. The club entered another competition and we were drawn to play at home against a leading league side, who were in a different class of cricket from us. We batted first and they put us out for 43. During the interval before they went out to bat most of the visitors began to get changed out of their flannels because they were so sure they wouldn't be required to go in. When my father went to see them only three were waiting in their whites. He advised them to get changed back again, pointing out that they were going to bat on a village green, not a league wicket. They laughed at him and said two of the men waiting to bat had scored centuries the week before.

'All right,' said Dad. 'But I've got a lad of fifteen here who might cause you a bit of trouble.'

I did just that. My analysis was six wickets for one run and they were all out for eleven. Afterwards the captain of their side came to my father and told him that I shouldn't be playing for a village side—I was too good. Dad told him to mind his own business and leave me alone because he considered me to be too young to move into higher grade cricket. But this fellow refused to keep quiet. He said they were going to be laughed to scorn when the news got around that his team had been thrashed by a village side, so he would have to let people know what had happened.

He went and told Cyril Turner, the former Yorkshire player who had been appointed coach to the Sheffield United Cricket Club. Cyril came to see me play. He and my father knew each other because they'd played together many years ago. After watching me for a bit he came to Dad and said: 'They call this lad Trueman. I suppose he's yours?' Dad said: 'Yes, he is. But he's not going anywhere yet, he's only fifteen.' Cyril ignored this. 'I want him in my nets next week,' he said—and there was no arguing with him.

By this time the whole family—Mother included—were coming to watch me play on Saturday afternoons. And when we got back home at night Dad would hold an inquest. If I'd done well I could tell he was very proud and happy but he never admitted it to me. Many's the time I knocked down five or six wickets and he'd tell me I'd been lucky to get more than two because the others came from bad deliveries. Then he would analyse my game, saying I would have got more wickets but I didn't put my left foot down properly, or my left arm was in the wrong position, or my chest was opening too early, or my run-up was too fast for accuracy. I used to sit there and take it all in, saying nowt. He never said anything about the possibility of my becoming a professional cricketer or playing for Yorkshire, but he must have privately nursed great hopes for me. I realize that now, but I didn't at the time. Personally I never gave the matter a thought. My ambition at that stage in my life was to become a bricklayer.

Chapter 2

County Cap

I didn't really know what county cricket was all about, since I'd never been to see any sort of match in that class, never even stepped on to a county ground. I read the papers I was delivering every morning and evening and knew about people like Hutton, Hammond, Sutcliffe and Leyland, but they were in another world. The first time I ever saw Test cricket was in 1947 when I went to the local picture house and there was a film report of the England versus South Africa match on Movietone News. I vividly remember a shot of this fielder running hard to make a good catch and then throwing the ball into the air. I thought to myself that it was a funny thing to do, because I'd never seen anything like that happen before. But I was most impressed and the next time a chance came my way in the field I tried to do the same. Trouble was I attempted to throw it in the air before I'd caught it properly and dropped the catch.

My brother Arthur was playing in the same team and he looked hard at me and said: 'You're trying to copy that fellow we saw at the pictures on Wednesday night, aren't you!' I felt a real fool. Incidentally it's a real pity that Arthur didn't try to become a professional cricketer himself, because he was good enough with the bat. But he was three years older than me, went off into the world on his own and forgot about cricket.

Me, I was just lucky. I went down to the nets at Sheffield to bowl for Cyril Turner and was most impressed by the ground, which, of course, was used regularly by Yorkshire. Cyril took me over, and I'll always owe him a lot because he was a superb coach. To begin with, he was amazed to see that I was holding the ball with my fingers across the seam. Nobody was ever able to explain how the hell I was managing to make the ball swing so much with a grip like that. Cyril taught me how to hold the ball properly and I was astonished to find out how much more there was to fast bowling than just running up and slinging the ball down. I began to learn how to make it swing both ways and how to follow through properly. I began to get seriously interested in the game for the first time, really wanted to become a good fast bowler. There had been no thought in my head until then about playing cricket for a living. In fact, it came as a great surprise to me when I learned that people actually got paid for playing.

In the meantime I'd left school and was working full time at delivering newspapers for a man called Tom Peel. It was a very big round and meant getting up at dawn to push papers through about 250 letter boxes, going round again with the evening editions, collecting the money every Friday and totting up the books. It was good money though—between seven and nine quid a week with tips. I did that for a year until one day Mother said that if I wanted to become a bricklayer it was time to get started. So a job was fixed for me with a building firm and I began working as an apprentice on a big site, building a new school on land behind the one I'd left at fourteen. I enjoyed the open air life but came up against a man who clearly did not like me. And the day came when I decided I must stand up to him. I spent all day wheeling enormous barrow loads of bricks to the brickies and this man tried to get me to load the barrows as well. I'm afraid I told him to bugger off, and I was promptly sacked. I got another job at Tinsley Wire Works in Sheffield making wall ties on a machine. I became very good at it but the work was very monotonous, so when I heard about good money to be made doing piece work at a glass works in Rotherham I went there. I made an awful lot of bottles in that place.

But cricket was looming larger and larger in my life by then and I couldn't wait for Saturdays to come round. Cyril Turner began playing me in Sheffield United's second team, and in my first match—the first ever league game for me—I took six wickets for eleven runs against English Steel Corporation. But Cyril didn't push things because he thought I was too young and I played quietly under his tuition for a year, learning all the time.

Now all league cricket in Yorkshire is geared to supply the needs of Yorkshire County Cricket Club, and coaches were expected to inform Headingley if they had any promising youngsters. Cyril was asked about new talent in Sheffield when they got round to picking the Yorkshire Federation tour side in 1948, which was for lads under eighteen. He told them he had a lad he thought would make a top-class quick bowler, but tried to resist when they asked him to send me to the Yorkshire nets for a look. He said he would rather hang on to me for a bit because I was only sixteen and not very big yet—only a touch over 5 ft. 4 in. But they insisted and a date was fixed. My father took the day off work and came along with me and Cyril. It was the first time I'd ever been to Leeds, and when I saw the Headingley ground I was stunned. The only field of that size I'd seen before had been full of turnips.

They took me to the nets and I bowled eleven balls, that's all. But I hit the stumps three times and one of the batsmen I beat was another youngster called Brian Close. Then the immortal George Herbert Hirst came and spoke to me. He was the man who set a record way back in 1906 which will never be beaten—200 wickets and 2,000 runs in one season. I'll never forget that conversation. He asked me my name and then inquired very keenly about where I came from. I told him I lived in Maltby but was born in Stainton. 'Is that in Yorkshire?' he asked. 'Oh yes,' I said, 'I'm Yorkshire born all right.' As any cricket follower knows, you can be the greatest cricketer ever to walk the earth, but if you aren't Yorkshire born you'll never play for the county. He then asked me if I was on my own and I told him my father and Cyril Turner were with me and I pointed out where my father was sitting. I followed him over and Dad stood up and took off his cap.

'This is Mr Hirst, Dad,' I said. 'Yes, I know who it is,' said Father, and shook hands with him.

I realized when he took his cap off that it was a great moment for him, but typically he never said anything about it afterwards. Mr Hirst told me to put on my coat, sit down and not move. He talked to Dad for a couple of minutes, then called over Cyril Turner and all three had a chat before walking off together and disappearing. For an hour and a half I sat there on my own wondering what the hell was going on, trying to work out what I'd done wrong. They had only let me bowl eleven times and not even asked to see me bat or field. On the other hand, I'd hit the wicket three times, which seemed reasonable. I was still worrying when my father reappeared. He was

27

very quiet—even for him—and after we'd had a bit of tea we went to get the bus home. He still said nothing for a long time and I was too scared to ask, but as the bus took us towards Doncaster he spoke up. 'It's going to cost me six pounds, but I don't care about that. You've been picked for the Federation tour and you're going.'

They sent the tour coach through Maltby to pick me up and Dad came with me as I walked down the lane, carrying my cricket bag and wearing a green sports jacket and grey flannels specially bought for the occasion. That night was the first I'd ever spent away from home and I slept in a dormitory at Harrow School, of all places. All the lads got on well together but I felt very sorry for one youngster because he was so travel sick on that coach. He said he was called Raymond Illingworth. Poor Ray, he still suffers the same way whenever you put him in a coach or a car. Brian Close was another on that tour and he was undoubtedly the star of the team. I believe he got a century when we played in Brighton. He was a big lad even as a teenager and he had bags of personality as well. I kept pretty quiet since I'd never experienced anything of this kind before. We played Buckinghamshire Colts in the first match, and next day they took us to watch Somerset play against Sussex. It was the first county match I'd ever seen and it was memorable because Harold Gimblett scored three hundred for Somerset. I fared reasonably well in the matches and managed to get four wickets one day. It was a happy fortnight and when I got off that coach at Maltby and waved them goodbye I got a big lump in my throat. I've always been an emotional sort of person, although most people refuse to believe it.

It was a good year for me, 1948. Cyril Turner promoted me to Sheffield's team in the Yorkshire Council league and at the end of the season one of my father's pals came to our house with a copy of the *Sheffield Telegraph*. There was a report of an after-dinner speech given by the legendary Herbert Sutcliffe, who had said there was a young man called Freddie Trueman who he predicted would play for Yorkshire before he was nineteen and for England before he was twenty-one. Now that was a great day in the Trueman household.

During the winter Yorkshire paid my travelling expenses to go to the indoor nets in Leeds and be coached by Bill Bowes and Arthur Mitchell. Brian Close was also invited, but not Ray Illingworth, who was trying to be a seam bowler then—the off-spinners didn't come until later in his career. Yorkshire then asked me to get a job in a reserved occupation to avoid conscription for National Service and remain available to play cricket. That meant only one thing where I lived—the pit. When I told Dad I wanted a job at Maltby Main he didn't know what to say because he had declared that no child of his would follow him down the mine. Earlier on my eldest brother Arthur had disobeyed him and it had broken his heart. After long discussions he agreed to get me a job in the tally office, which meant I didn't have to do the rough work at the coal face like him. But I often went down to find which seam he was working and spend fifteen minutes or so shovelling coal on to the belts so that he could sit down and have a rest. The old man was over fifty then and still slogging away.

But it's still not accurate to say—as many have—that I built up my strength by manual labour down the pit. The truth is I was blessed with two things from birth— the Trueman tenacity and a perfect physique for a fast bowler. I always had strong, thick legs—those are the first essentials for quick bowling—big shoulders and hips.

I got on well at the pit and worked there all through the winter. The 1949 season arrived and with it, one Friday morning in early May, a Post Office boy tapping on the door with a telegram. It was from Headingley. I had been picked to play for Yorkshire against Cambridge University. Dad didn't see it until he came home from work in the evening, and again he kept his emotions hidden and said nothing. Instead he immediately set about getting some equipment for me because I had none of my own. He borrowed a bat, a big heavy thing, from the colliery cricket club and I managed to find someone with a pair of batting gloves to lend. He knew I wasn't going to be able to share with the rest of the team for this match. On the Monday he took me to Doncaster to buy some new clothes. That set him back more than £20 and he said I would have to pay him back now that I was working.

I joined the team coach at the Danum Hotel, Doncaster, and met up again with Brian Close, who was also making his debut for Yorkshire along with a young opening bat called Frank Lowson. Brian was the only person in the party I'd ever met before and I must say I felt over-awed and a bit awkward. I didn't touch alcohol in those days so there was a bit of a laugh when I ordered orange juice, and then I was worried over what they would say about the pipe I was smoking. I never touched cigarettes—I didn't dare. When my brother Arthur was nineteen he came into our house with a cigarette in his mouth and Father jumped up and knocked it clean out of his mouth. I was sixteen at the time and I thought, 'Good Lord, he'll kill me if he finds out I smoke a pipe'.

Not long afterwards I came home smoking my pipe to find Dad sitting there in his chair when he should have been at work. There had been some trouble at the pit. Anyway, it was too late to hide the thing so I just sat back and waited for a belt in the earhole. Eventually he folded his paper, took off his glasses and said: 'How long have you been smoking a pipe?' I told him the truth—since I was sixteen. 'Oh well,' he said. 'If you smoke a pipe you won't go far wrong.' He always smoked one himself.

I was just as relieved when the Yorkshire officials didn't seem concerned about the pipe as we drove towards Fenners, and further relief came when I got an early wicket. Cambridge batted first and I was bowling against a chap called Morris when I was asked if I could bowl a bouncer because opinion agreed that was the way to get him out. They didn't need to ask! So I bowled my first ever bouncer in first-class cricket and he fended it off short straight into the hands of short leg. I ended the match with two more wickets, feeling reasonably satisfied with myself, and in the next match against Oxford University did even better. I got four quick wickets and heard old Denis Hendren, the umpire, say that if Freddie Trueman didn't end up playing for England, then he was no umpire. I know I was very tired at the end of each day and got blisters running around in an outfield far bigger than anything I'd ever played on before. One night I went to bed at nine o'clock, exhausted.

Brian Close and Frank Lowson were chosen for the next match, but I wasn't. That didn't really worry me. I was only too happy to have actually played for Yorkshire because I had enough intelligence to realize that I could now build a platform for a living. Until that match I still hadn't been able to bring myself to believe that cricket would become a full-time career. But once you had played for the first team, Yorkshire automatically gave you your second team cap and blazer, which was good enough to establish you as a professional cricketer in Yorkshire. As it happened, I was to play only four times for the second team. I also had enough nous to know that my bowling action was nowhere near right and it came as no surprise to be dropped, since Yorkshire already had Ron Aspinall, who was good enough to bowl for England, and Alex Coxon to lead their pace attack. I wasn't bowling as straight as I should because at that time I had too much swing and not enough speed. Even so, for someone of my pace I moved the ball a long way, often aiming at off and middle and missing the off stump by nine inches. I could also pitch at the leg stump and catch the outside edge of the off. This swing was the reason for my success later on when I built up speed and still kept the swing, only more controlled. I just couldn't miss getting wickets. I reckon that I probably moved the ball more than any other pace bowler in the history of the game, and what's more I could make the ball swing away from the bat. That's the one which shifts even the great batsmen. The inswinger they can usually deal with, but the outswinger is the one which always gets them into trouble eventually. They are forced to adjust their bat to it and risk giving an edge.

So I worked on building speed and improving my run-up throughout 1949 and 1950 and became convinced that I was going to win in the end. I was in and out—mostly out—of the Yorkshire team and when picked was probably trying too hard to make an impression. I recall one disastrous match at Bramall Lane, Sheffield, against the New Zealanders when the entire family and many Maltby and Stainton folk turned up to watch me play for

Yorkshire. I was so anxious not to let them down that I went at it like a bull at a gate and damaged a thigh muscle so badly that they carried me off and I couldn't play for weeks. Still, I was a happy man and totally unaware of what was supposed to be going on behind the scenes at Yorkshire. It has been said—and written—that some of the influential people at Headingley considered me too wild and inaccurate ever to make a Yorkshire player, despite what the coaches said about my 'superb, natural action'. No one said anything to me and for my part I was already convinced that I was to become the best and fastest bowler in the land. I knew they were trying out other young pacemen, but when I watched them I came to the conclusion that I had nothing to worry about.

I was certainly happy about the money I was earning. After the university tour they gave me £40—more cash than I'd ever seen in my life. I paid my father back what I owed him and had enough left over to buy a decent pipe and change to a better brand of tobacco. And when Yorkshire didn't want me, there were plenty of league clubs which did, midweek and weekends. They were prepared to pay me £10 to £15, and I could pick up more with a collection if I did well. I frightened a few batsmen in those matches.

I bought a few more clothes too, and this led to the first crop of ridiculous stories about me. They said I was turning up to Yorkshire's nets wearing loud clothes, and ties with pictures of naked women painted on. Let me tell you that if I'd ever put on a tie like that my father would have got hold of me and tied it so tight I'd never have breathed again, never mind bowled. He was very keen about being properly dressed.

In the 1949 and 1950 seasons I collected a total of 62

wickets for Yorkshire and even got picked to play for the Rest against England in a Test trial in 1950, long before I began to play regularly for my county. I didn't fare too badly either. But when 1951 arrived I was certain that the field was clear for me. There just were no quick bowlers in England, never mind Yorkshire, apart from Les Jackson of Derbyshire who was, in my opinion, probably the most underrated fast bowler that ever played cricket. I'm sure that if he'd played for any other county he would have been an automatic choice for England. But there were those in the hierarchy who said they didn't like his action, although they really knew damn all about the game. I played about twenty matches for Yorkshire in 1951 and took 90 wickets. And began to make enemies. Before I arrived, opening batsmen were having it easy, able to play off their front foot without a care in the world. Now, if a batsman started playing forward to me before I'd even delivered the ball there was every chance he would find it whistling round his ears. They didn't like it. I wasn't trying to hurt them— just forcing them to go on their back foot and play a little—but inevitably one or two got hit. I was sorry when this happened but I never allowed myself to show it. Batsmen were my natural enemy. Some of them began to call me names, which was the worst thing they could do. I'm a retaliator by nature, so the more they prattled on, the more the ball bounced, since an unsettled batsman is easier to get out.

But trouble with batsmen was nothing compared to what I came up against when I landed a fairly regular place with Yorkshire. I could scarcely credit it, because I found that though cricket may be the greatest game in the world, it is also the most vicious, two-faced, back-stabbing game ever invented. And I really walked into it, an innocent. To begin with, the Yorkshire dressing-room in the 1950s was not a happy place. It shows in the records. We had great names like Len Hutton, Wardle, Yardley, Close and Appleyard and we hardly seemed to win a damned thing in ten years. The team was split into rival cliques, with the senior players like Hutton and Yardley and the amateurs going their way—even staying at different hotels—and the youngsters like Close, Lowson and myself out in the cold. There was terrible jealousy between the groups, and the younger players quickly learned never to approach the seniors for help. Ray Illingworth once went to Len Hutton for advice and came out in great distress. Even at international level, youngsters in the game would be crucified. Brian Close is the strongest and hardest man I've ever known, but when he went on his first tour of Australia at the age of nineteen he spent nights alone in his room, heart-broken. I understand he finally lost his temper and gave one of the golden boys of England cricket a bloody good hiding. Another mate of mine gave the same player a thrashing in a festival match and never played for Yorkshire again.

I came up against the Yorkshire spin bowlers who had it all their own way, enjoying a lot of wickets before I came along. There was one occasion in 1951 when I was sitting in the bath feeling very pleased with myself after taking seven wickets on a batter's wicket in Bradford. Suddenly I heard a big rumpus coming from the dressing-room. I got dried and dressed and went to find out what was going on and was told by Johnny Whitehead, one of the younger players, that he'd just spoken his mind. One of the seniors, a noted England spin bowler, had announced that Trueman had been 'bloody lucky' to get all those wickets. Johnny had lost his temper and

35

gone for him. There was trouble and bad temper all the time. When the juniors were doing well we got it in the neck, and when we made mistakes the roof fell in. If, say, Frank Lowson accidentally ran out Len Hutton there was hell to pay for weeks, not just from the seniors but from the newspapers in Yorkshire, who rated the running out of Len a crime roughly equivalent to murder. Everything that went wrong was our fault. Even if one of our lot got a good score, he was accused of playing for himself and not for the team.

The uncapped players also had all the running around to do for the seniors, which I didn't mind because I believed it was good training. We had to fetch drinks and lunches for them, collect their cricket bags and see them safely transported on away trips. When we arrived at a station, we organized porters to carry the bags, got two taxis, found the money to pay for them, gave out tips and got everything to the ground. But there were times when a senior would tell us to 'bugger off' and refuse to pay his share. More than once we were owed over £5—a lot of money to us—and Norman Yardley, the skipper, had to threaten to stop it out of their match money if they didn't pay up. Not many people realize that Yorkshire players had to pay all their own expenses—travelling, hotels, meals, the lot. Many of them stayed in cheap hotels and nipped round the corner for a bag of fish and chips at nights. I always lashed out for a good meal, however, because I had the sense to realize that you can't bowl fast on a diet of cheap snacks.

Apart from the atmosphere in the dressing-room, we also had to put up with real hostility from the other counties. Now keen competition is a healthy thing, but Yorkshire were genuinely hated. Apparently this stemmed from the time between the wars, when the

Yorkshire team beat everybody in sight and then went on to cause havoc off the ground. Some of the things they were supposed to have done defy description, and I also heard about fantastic brawls in hotels and pubs. There was still one hotel in Swansea which wouldn't let a Yorkshire player through the doors. The coaches to the teams we were meeting had been players themselves during that era and they passed on their feelings to the men they trained. Of course, nobody marked my card and it took me some time to realize that the seniors were making the bullets and getting me to fire them. There was a lot of bitterness between Yorkshire and Middlesex and a feud went on for years between the big names on these two sides. They were jealous as hell of each other.

When I cottoned on to what was happening I told them to do their own dirty work and started to stay out of everyone's way, keep my mouth shut and try to avoid trouble. But by then I had already acquired a bad name and there was no way to stop the jealousy. I began to get free suits, shirts, shoes and occasionally gifts of money for particularly good performances from wealthy supporters who were delighted to see a really quick bowler playing for Yorkshire again, and that didn't go down well at all. But I can still hardly believe what happened to me in 1954 when we were playing Kent at Dover and giving them a real beating. I had taken all the first eight wickets for under twenty runs and was set for taking all ten. Now there was a special prize of one hundred guineas and the Brylcreem Silver Cup to any bowler taking ten in an innings and I say to this day that two of my supposed team mates deliberately dropped catches to stop me getting it. It was one of the few times I became really nasty, and when we arrived back in the dressing-room one grand old Yorkshire supporter came in and told one player his opinion about a missed catch. Then he turned to me and said, 'Don't worry, Freddie. You're still going to get the hundred guineas,' took out his cheque-book and wrote out a cheque there and then. When he left the others suggested that I should share out the money and I told them exactly where to go.

All through these disturbances I was trying to concentrate on becoming a successful fast bowler. I really worked at it, studying how I could get batsmen out. There are four basic things a batter can do—play forward, back, hit on the offside and hit on the onside. I realized that if you could induce him to enter no-man's-land between these four areas you stood a chance of nailing him. I also worked at my fielding to play myself into a close-to-the-wicket position, and for most of my career fielded at leg slip or short leg. There I could watch closely how various batsmen reacted, particularly when they were playing pace. I've been blessed with a near-photographic memory, so I gradually built up a mental filing system about nearly every batsman in the land. I watched how they moved, where they placed their feet as the bowler ran up, and tried to calculate their strengths and weaknesses—and how to exploit the weaknesses. If a batsman was a very good back-foot player and I noticed he was going on to his back foot before delivery, I would pitch the ball up another foot and try to make it swing a little later. If he liked to play off his front foot, I would pitch short. If a man was weak on the onside I would pitch at the leg stump, and vice versa.

By the middle of the 1951 season my patience was wearing thin with Yorkshire. I began to think I would never get anywhere. I would bowl well and get plenty of wickets in one match and get dropped for the next. There was no mention of being capped. Apart from the honour, which was considerable, a capped player was paid an extra £2 a match, plus a monthly retainer. There was one notable occasion when we played against Nottingham at Sheffield and all the Trueman family and friends turned out in force again. I had a second innings analysis of 8 for 68 and we beat them by an innings. The crowd cheered me all the way to the dressing-room, where I found that I had been dropped to the second team for the next match. And I didn't even play in that. They made me twelfth man and I was roasted for falling asleep in a deck-chair during play.

In the end I virtually had to ask for my cap. Both Lancashire and Surrey were making overtures and I came to the conclusion that to make any progress in cricket I would have to leave Yorkshire. So I went to Norman Yardley and told him I was going. That was midweek —and on the following Monday, 13 August, I got my cap. There was no warning and no ceremony. We were playing at Bradford when Norman Yardley told Bob Appleyard and myself to go to the office. When we got there he just handed over caps. I couldn't wait to get home, but in those days I had no car and was travelling by train and bus to the ground and back to save hotel bills, arriving home at ten o'clock at night. When I got into the house I saw my old Dad sitting in his chair. Now he was on the night shift in those days but, of course, the news had already reached Maltby via the newspapers and I knew what was up. I decided to have a bit of fun, saying, 'What's the matter, then? Last draw at the mine was 9.30 p.m. and here you are still at home at ten o'clock.' Well, his face puckered and I thought, 'Good God! He's going to cry.' Then he pulled himself together and said: 'On a night like this in a Yorkshireman's life, he doesn't go to work.' He looked me full in the face and said, 'Come on, where is it?' So I took my cap out and gave it to him.

I'll never be able to describe properly just what it meant to him, that cap. Only Yorkshiremen will understand. I never wore it again—it was his, and he'd worked for it. Mother was watching all this from the kitchen, so I turned to her and said, 'Don't worry, Mum, you can have my first England cap.' And she burst into tears. She got it too, but Dad never bothered about my England caps. They meant nothing to him. That Yorkshire cap was all he wanted and he still has it.

When he died it was placed in his coffin.

Chapter 3

The White English Bastard

Just before I got that cap, the Yorkshire Committee made a ruling that any capped players called up to do National Service would be paid £5 a week. So at the end of the season in which I got mine I said to hell with the pit and quit, which meant I made myself liable for call-up. I didn't want to stop playing for Yorkshire but I had to get it over and done with. I went for my medical on the afternoon of the day we beat Essex before lunch and I decided to make an attempt to swing it by pretending to be colour blind. But the medic who tested my eyesight laughed me out of court. He said, 'I saw you take a brilliant catch at leg slip today, and if you can spot a cricket ball travelling at that speed there's nothing wrong with your eyes.' So I was in, classified A1. I never got away with anything.

But I must say I enjoyed the forces, square-bashing, spud-bashing, the lot. I was brought up to respond to discipline and never objected to it in my life when it was properly applied and had some purpose. They put me in the Royal Air Force, and after basic training I got posted to Hemswell in Lincolnshire, which was not only handily placed—only thirty-two miles away from home—but was commanded by a marvellous man called Jim Warfield, a group captain and a real cricket enthusiast. He put me in the sports section looking after equipment, and if Yorkshire wanted me for the odd match he would always agree, providing they had a proper reason. I also played a lot of cricket for the station, the RAF and the Combined Services, and kept fit in the winter by playing soccer. I wasn't bad at that either, and Lincoln City were impressed enough to offer me terms.

Those two years in the RAF were not wasted for me. I certainly matured physically, putting on two or three vital inches in height and even more round the chest. Someone likened me to a Spanish fighting bull, which was about right. I stood 5 ft. 10 in., weighed $13\frac{1}{2}$ stone, measured 46 in. round chest and hips and 19 in. round the thighs. I didn't alter much during my entire playing career. And I had the confidence to match my strength. I knew I was going to be the best fast bowler Yorkshire had ever produced—that may be an immodest thing to say, but there was never any question in my mind from then on. I also knew I would play for England. Australia had humiliated us in Test Match after Test Match because they had two great fast bowlers—well, one anyway. Lindwall was among the best ever and Miller was pretty good too. But we had none worth speaking of and the need to find bowlers who could retaliate by frightening the Aussies was the only thing the cricket writers in the newspapers could think about. They went on about it as though it was a national emergency, which I suppose it was. They say the moment maketh the man, and I knew that man was me. I remember a big newspaper article in 1952 which said that if the answer to England's fast bowling problem was in the forces, then arrangements must be made for his release. I read all this, kept quiet and dished out footballs and cricket bats to my fellow erks. Then Yorkshire applied to have me released for two weeks just before the start of a Test series with India, which I later realized was probably fixed by the England selectors so that they could have a look at me. I was fit and ready. I set about Somerset at Huddersfield and bowled them out, gave Worcester a hell of a hammering at Bradford and put out Derbyshire at Sheffield. Everything went magnificently and I returned to the sports store feeling that I may have proved something at last. But it still came as a shock when I was selected for my first Test because I wasn't, after all, playing regularly in first-class cricket. The day it happened I was in the sports store when the phone rang and a strange voice said: 'What do you think about being picked for England next Thursday?' I said, 'Oh, bollocks!' and slammed the phone down. You see, I was used to getting daft calls ever since my name had started figuring in the newspapers. Anyway, the same man called again so I gave him a right rollicking and told him to stop bothering me. When it rang for the third time a warrant officer picked it up and told me that a man called Bill Bowes wanted to speak to me. The man who had been on before was a *Yorkshire Post* reporter called John Bapty, who used to travel around with the county side and he had brought Bill to the phone to convince me it wasn't a hoax. I still wouldn't believe it for a bit, but when the news sank in I went—more like floated on air— to see Group Captain Warfield to tell him and see if he would give me the time off. He said jokingly he would agree on one condition—if he could have complimentary tickets for himself and his wife!

I soon fixed that and on the night before the Test turned up at the Prince of Wales Hotel in Harrogate to attend the traditional pre-match dinner. It was a bit nerve-racking, mixing with all the big names like Compton, Edrich and Hutton who had all been scoring centuries for England before the war, when I was a babe in arms. They didn't spend much time talking to me, and when I went to bed couldn't get to sleep as easily as normal because I worried about finishing up as twelfth man when they announced the team next morning. I tried to convince myself that Len Hutton, just appointed as England's first professional captain, would drop a batsman. But it came as an enormous relief next day when I made the eleven, mostly because I had promised Mother my cap and I didn't want to let her down. It was, of course, a great thrill, heightened by the fact I was playing in front of my own crowd at Headingley, but I must confess that the edge was taken off the occasion because I'd just finished a really tight and exciting game against our traditional rivals, Lancashire, and there just wasn't the same atmosphere playing against India. It would have been altogether different if we had been up against Australia.

India batted first and I was a bit put out when the Kirkstall Road end with its downhill run was given to Alec Bedser. That was usually mine. I had to come up the hill from the Headingley end and needed to push my run to counteract it until it flattened out, which disturbed my rhythm. I reckon Len Hutton made a mistake there, really, because I was two yards faster than Bedser. I remember desperately wanting to make history by getting a wicket with the first ball I ever bowled in Test cricket, but that was one record I had to do without. In fact, I had to wait until my second spell for that first wicket when Polly Umrigar came in at No. 3. Len reasoned that he didn't like speed, so he set me at him, and the skipper was absolutely right. He jabbed at one delivery and edged it into the gloves of Godfrey Evans behind the wicket. I got two more prime wickets in that innings and conceded 89 runs. Not exactly a dream start to a Test career, but it had to do.

But I did make history when India came in for their second innings. It was probably the most sensational start to any Test innings. This time Len let me bowl down the hill, so I got the chance to show that England had got a really quick bowler at last. Roy scooped my second ball into the hands of Denis Compton and then Bedser had Gaekwad caught in the gully without a run being put on the board. For some reason India sent in their wicket keeper, Mantri, and I decided to vary things by giving him a slower delivery. I wasn't great at hiding it but I could do it, and not the way some of the older fast bowlers told me either—that is, bowl at the same pace but release the ball behind the crease. Some of those old-timers talked a load of old cock and I worked out my own way of doing it, as usual. The idea is to make the batsman play early, and that ball I put down to Mantri is one I will never forget—the sort all fast bowlers dream about. It pitched on his middle stump, straightened out and knocked his off stump clean out of the ground. Three wickets for no runs! When I bowled out Manjrekar with the next delivery I could scarcely believe it myself. Four for none, and the crowd going out of their minds. A hat trick in my very first Test was probably too much to ask and I missed it—by a whisker. It was so fast I don't think Hazare saw it until Godfrey Evans was chucking it back.

We murdered India that summer and I ended up with 29 Test wickets, including 8 for 31 in less than nine overs in the Third Test at Old Trafford, which I never bettered. Neither did anyone else, for that matter. The press went overboard and I collected more headlines in a couple of months than some cricketers get in a lifetime. So there I was, a lad of twenty-one from a working-class background hailed as the new white bowling hope. The trouble started from then—started as soon as I got back to camp after the first Test, in fact. There was a bit of resentment about my getting yet another week's extra leave. The officers were all right but some of the NCOs tried to take advantage and I just told them to get stuffed. I managed to avoid nasty situations by just walking on when they tried to be stupid, but there was one occasion coming back on the bus from Lincoln after a night out when somebody tried to have a go at me. The bus was pretty full and I had nipped off to get some fish and chips for my mates. They were trying to save my seat for me when this idiot started shouting about it and when I got back asked me who the hell I thought I was. He knew exactly who I was, of course, which I suppose was what it was really all about. He wouldn't listen to the explanation and went on so much that I jumped up to let him have one. Two of my mates rushed in and kept us apart, which was just as well because I got so mad at some of the things he was saying that I would have hospitalized him.

It came at me from all sides after that first Test series. Some people began saying that Freddie Trueman's rise to fame had been too rapid and I needed cutting down to size. This I could stand, but the real shock was the total loss of my privacy—it took me years to get used to that. I found I couldn't go into a pub without someone starting to say provocative things in a loud voice or coming right up to me to tell me that his mate farther down the bar would have made a far quicker and better bowler than me if only he had taken up cricket seriously. The world seemed to be full of lunatics all of a sudden.

And then I couldn't go and have a quiet meal in a

restaurant with a girl friend without someone slamming an autograph book—or, more often, a bit of scrap paper —and demanding my signature. Not asking politely— demanding. I had been brought up to behave differently, so I would say, 'Do you mind? Firstly, I'm having my meal—secondly, in the humble home I come from I was taught to say please and thank you. Get lost!' So I began to acquire a reputation for rudeness. Although I have always been prepared to sign anyone's autograph when the request is made properly and in a reasonable place, it's a pain in the backside most of the time. I'm not alone in thinking this. I remember once in 1952 during a Test match I was at a table in a London hotel with Len Hutton and Willie Watson talking to Arthur Askey when a fellow came with about five autograph books, slapped them down on the table in front of Arthur and said: 'Here, sign these!' Arthur just picked them up and threw them on the floor without pausing in his conversation. It came as a big relief to find that other people much more experienced at being in the public eye resented it.

One thing I did enjoy, though, was the money. I was being paid all over the place—£5 a week from Yorkshire for doing my National Service, plus match fees when I played, about a tenner a week for playing for Leeds in the Yorkshire Council league on Saturdays and quite a bit more for making personal appearances. I didn't even bother to draw my pay every week as an Aircraftman First Class. The first time I went on a pay parade, I queued up, snapped off a salute, shouted my number and a very young officer pushed eighteen shillings across the table to me. When he saw me looking at it somewhat askance, he said, 'What's the matter, Trueman? Isn't it enough?' I answered, 'It will have to be, sir!' and went straight to the pay office to arrange to draw the

47

rest of my pay in a lump sum when I was due to be demobbed in September 1953.

I still only got £238 for two years' work and cricket in the RAF, but I'm not complaining because they were pretty good to me. It brought my bank balance up to £2,800, which wasn't bad at twenty-one for a miner's son from Maltby. Mind, I wasn't extravagant with my brass, although I had begun to take the occasional pint of beer for the first time in my life, basically to be sociable. And during the last year of service life I splashed out on my first car. I'd spotted one advertised on the other side of Maltby, a little 1932 MG with a fabric-covered body and a bumble-bee backside. A man and his son were asking £75 for it, so I didn't argue and paid up, getting £2 luck money back. Then I got into the thing and said, 'Right—what do I do?' Well, they boggled at me and the old man said, 'Bloody 'ell, can't you drive?' I said that I couldn't, and since they didn't want to give me my money back they showed me how to work the gears and the clutch and off I went. I wasn't that ignorant about the art of driving because I had carefully watched other people. I drove that car thirty-four miles back to camp without trouble or incident. But when I arrived a good pal of mine called Pete Varley—he's in America now, running his own haulage and transport business—blew his top when I told him what I had done and gave me a right bollocking, which I deserved. So I got some L-plates and Pete taught me the finer points of driving, and if he couldn't help I used to practise round the perimeter of the airfield when the planes were grounded. Six weeks later I passed my test first time.

There were other Tests that year too—but I failed to make most of those. The Australians came over and I wasn't picked until the last Test at the Oval, although

I was called to the Old Trafford Test and sat it out on
the sidelines as twelfth man. All the other four matches
had been drawn, so this was the vital one, since we had a
chance of getting back the Ashes after many years of
losing. As any cricket fan will tell you, that Test became
one of the most glorious moments in English cricket
history because we beat them by eight wickets. The
crowd stood round the pavilion in their thousands at the
finish, shouting and cheering. I got 4 wickets for 86, so I
made a fair contribution. I also got a very sore shoulder
because Ray Lindwall violated the truce that exists
between fast bowlers and let me have a bouncer. It hit
my shoulder blade so hard that I thought someone had
stuck a knife in it, but I didn't let him know he'd hurt
me. I just made a mental note to pay him back and had
to wait five years before the chance came. He faced up
to me in the second Test at Melbourne in the 1958–9
series and I gave him one which reared up, struck his
bat handle, clouted him between the eyes and flew up
into the air to give a simple catch. Ray came to me after
the match to complain and started going on about his
age, so I told him that I didn't squeal when he did me at
the Oval. 'Christ!' he said. 'Do you remember that?'
I said that I certainly did. 'Okay, come and have a
drink on me,' he said. Keith Miller also bowled bouncers
at me—twice—and he was another who got paid back
in the end.

I was still in the RAF when they picked me for the MCC
tour of the West Indies in the winter of 1953–4. In retro-
spect I think it may have been better for my subsequent
career had I been passed over. I was still just a lad of
twenty-one who hadn't been any farther than Cleethorpes except with a cricket team, and everyone made

the mistake of thinking that I was going to murder the West Indians. Yet I had still to play a full season in county cricket, I hadn't been able to train properly in the RAF and was unfit in the cricketing sense. And if they had thought of looking up the records it would have been obvious to anyone that the wickets out there are a paradise for batsmen and the worst in the world for fast bowlers. The first triple century in cricket history had been scored in Jamaica around 1912 and they had gone on from there, knocking up massive totals year in year out. Anyone who can bat well is going to get runs in the West Indies. I was upset before we even set off because Lennox-Boyd, who was the Colonial Secretary then, came to have dinner with us and tell us to be careful for political reasons, not to upset public opinion over there. Well, I already knew I was going there to sweat my guts out in the sun for several months and come back with around £200 after tax, so I upped and said that if I was expected to be a diplomat I should be paid like one and get diplomatic privileges. And then something else happened which I really objected to—it was made clear by Len Hutton that we should not fraternize with the West Indian cricketers. I had met people like Frank Worrell, Clyde Walcott and Everton Weekes regularly in league cricket in England and there was no way I was going to ignore them.

Now in my opinion Len Hutton was the greatest player I ever saw, far and away the best batsman in the world and a marvellous tactician as a captain. But to my mind he wasn't much good off the field, particularly at backing his players up when necessary. On that tour it seemed that you just couldn't approach him to try to sort things out when trouble came. And it did. Some of it was just accidental, such as the time I broke George Headley's arm in Jamaica, which the local fans and press naturally didn't like overmuch. I was very sorry about it because George was one of my cricketing idols, a great batsman who used to be called the Black Bradman, although in the West Indies Bradman was known as the White Headley! He was a bit past it at the time—he was over forty.

There's no doubt that the incident did me no good, and my image wasn't helped by a load of bilge the press were writing about me, calling me 'Fiery Fred', 'Terrible Trueman' and the 'Maltby Mauler'. The West Indians took this up and even wrote a calypso about me bowling bumpers. So anything that happened after that was generally blamed on me. The worst example came in Georgetown when one of the umpires complained to Len that he had been called 'a black bastard'. Len gave me such a terrible verbal hiding back in the dressing-room in front of all the other players that I asked Charlie Palmer, the tour manager, if I could go home there and then. The next morning I met that umpire at the top of the pavilion steps and asked him why he had told Len I had called him a black bastard. And he said, 'I didn't— I said it was one of the Yorkshiremen on the field, but I know it wasn't you.' Well, there were four Yorkshiremen on that field, including Len, so I took that umpire into our dressing-room and confronted Len, who said words to the effect that the incident was closed. But I said it bloody well wasn't and made him listen to what the umpire had to say. The other lads went mad. You see, there had just been an incident at an hotel in Barbados which had unjustifiably been blamed on me. But Len didn't apologize and nothing changed.

In another match Tom Graveney held a perfectly good catch in the slips and the umpire gave not out, so in exasperation he threw the ball into the ground—we had been suffering from some bad umpiring. At a cocktail party after the match some pompous idiot came up to me and said: 'Well, Trueman, I hear you've been at it again today, throwing the ball into the ground and disputing the umpire's decision.' Fortunately Tom heard this, whipped round and snarled: 'No! Not him—me!' I was so grateful to hear someone sticking up for me at last and I felt quite sorry for once trying to knock Tom's head off at Sheffield for appealing against the light. There was another incident at Georgetown when Denis Compton picked up one of the bottles the crowd had thrown on the ground and lobbed it back at them. If that had been me I would have been on the next banana boat home, no question.

But the biggest row on that tour came when I was doing some stock, fast medium bowling in a minor match deputizing for someone who had been injured. I put one just short of a length to a man who is now dead and gone —and he called me a white English bastard. I told him that if he said that again I would bloody do him. A couple of overs later he did say it again so I gave him a bouncer which put him in hospital with a broken jaw and several teeth missing. I was so mad, I didn't go to him but walked back to the start of my run-up and sat down. I refused to apologize to him unless he apologized to me. I still say he asked for it, although I rarely enjoyed hurting anyone.

It was not a happy tour for me at all, although I certainly didn't disgrace myself. In the first-class matches I took 27 wickets—more than anyone except Tony Lock, who got 28—and sweated through 320 overs. But I really fell out with some of the older, established stars in our team who amazed me with their behaviour. They were getting away with murder, including coming back regularly at two and three in the morning stoned out of their minds and waking everyone up. I resented this because I needed my rest, and I also resented it when Tony Lock and I got the blame for their antics, so I told them what I thought of them to their faces. They didn't like it, of course, and there were one or two scenes.

I put most of the blame for the treatment I experienced in the West Indies on Len Hutton, but there is no doubt that he was having problems with the same experienced and established stars, nearly all of whom played for the southern counties. I believe they resented him not just because he was so much better than them, but because he was a Yorkshireman *and* the first professional captain of England. Since they couldn't get at him because he was in charge, I was the obvious target. But I felt I got little support from Len, who scarcely seemed to talk to anyone and went his own way. I was furious when my good conduct bonus was stopped and he refused to tell me why, and still refused when I asked him more than ten years later. I was the only one punished in this way despite all the riotous goings-on and drunkenness of which I had no part. Despite all the stories that are told about me, I can truthfully say that I've never been drunk in my life.

Worse still, the word went round when we returned to England that Len Hutton couldn't control me. So the big guns of the MCC like Freddie Brown and Gubby Allen, along with Brian Sellers, chairman of Yorkshire, decided they were going to sort me out and tame me. Bill Bowes once told me that an MCC committee member came up to him and said, 'My word, this Trueman's a bad-tempered devil, isn't he!' Bill said, 'No, I don't think so—have you ever met him?' The man admitted that he hadn't, so Bill asked him how the hell he could form such an opinion. But the maverick label stuck and when Len Hutton and the selectors announced the team to tour Australia next winter, I wasn't in it. During the summer I'd taken 134 wickets for under 16 runs apiece, but they decided that wasn't good enough and took five other pace bowlers instead. They also passed me over for the Tests against Pakistan the same year. It was a terrible blow and it has been reported that I swore I would never play for England again, if asked. That wasn't strictly true—I said it made me feel like saying I would never play again.

The fact is I was never asked to play for England again under Len Hutton's captaincy. I'll never be able to forgive either Len or the MCC for that.

Chapter 4

Resentments and a Spot of Bother

Herbert Sutcliffe was absolutely right when he said that some batsmen can play fast bowling and some cannot, but if they all told the truth none of them like it. Now I happened to be the first really fast bowler to come along in English cricket for many years, and I am convinced that the ridiculous image conferred upon me was partly to do with that. If someone else had arrived before or at the same time, there would have been another to share the shrapnel that burst around my head. I was playing in a Test trial before Brian Statham had even appeared for Lancashire, and Frank Tyson didn't come on the scene for years. Now Brian and I bowled in harness for England for a long time and he was a very quick bowler —and a firm friend of mine, despite the rumours that we didn't get on—yet Brian was always the blue-eyed boy and I was always the villain, whatever happened. And the thing that exaggerated the situation was the advent of television, which created an altogether new interest in sport and sportsmen. Suddenly we were all performing in the corner of every living-room in the land, and this unleashed a surge of press interest in personalities. In my early days there would only be a handful of reporters turning up for matches and they were interested in the game. By the middle fifties there were platoons of them, all trying to find a different story—and it didn't necessarily have to do with cricket. Or with the truth, for that matter.

I became the natural target because I had returned from the West Indies in supposed disgrace. They set me up as the untameable northern savage who ate broken glass and infant batsmen for breakfast. Of course I was aggressive on the field and I suppose I looked it. But I reasoned that you can't act like a pansy and be respected as a fast bowler, and batsmen were there to be got out as soon as possible. If the odd bouncer helped to break their concentration—and that is what I was trying to break, not their skulls—then I considered it a fair weapon. I didn't play cricket for social reasons like some of the fancy amateurs. It was my living and I played to win. On the field the other team were my enemies and you could keep the old pals act until we went into the bar after the match. Unfortunately some of the people I bowled against seemed to take it personally. They used to come up to me in the pavilion and say, 'You tried to bloody hit me today, Trueman!' I always said the same thing in reply: 'Don't be so daft—I'd rather bowl you out. If I hit you and you are carried off, then I can't get your wicket, can I?'

Of course, what helped to anger and confuse them was another new ingredient I brought to the county game— the ability to bowl outswingers consistently. Very few quick bowlers in the history of the game could bowl a genuine outswinger and mean it. I have no idea why— all I know is that I could bowl them naturally from the age of about eight, when I didn't even know what they were. And I never forgot those days back in the Yorkshire nets when I was a youngster trying to make the grade, and the immortal Maurice Leyland saying to me: 'Keep bowling those outswingers, Fred, and you'll be all right. That's the one which gets the great players out!' That ability was really the secret of my success. Ray Lindwall could bowl them and so could Wes Hall, but the other English fast bowlers of my generation could not. Brian Statham could make the ball come back in off the wicket but would be the first to tell you that he couldn't intentionally swing the ball—in other words, make it curve in the air—and Frank Tyson was just quick and straight.

The outswinger is a delivery bowled basically from close to the stumps and aimed to pitch around leg and middle and move towards the off stump. Only sideways-on bowlers can make the ball swing away—and cricket is really a sideways-on game, although you would scarcely believe it on today's evidence. As you deliver it your left elbow must point towards fine leg, which brings your left shoulder in line with the wickets and batsman, and as your left foot goes across you must swivel from the hips and on the ball of the left foot as it hits the floor so that the whole of your body comes round as the ball is released. It is also necessary to drag the back foot instead of picking it up to help you get round. So many fast bowlers today land on their heel, which is why they get such a lot of leg trouble. I bowled for twenty years without even pulling a muscle, which was entirely due to my correct action. The inswinger, which moves from off to leg, is a different action altogether. I was never a natural at the inswinger, but I could move the ball back off the seam to leg by opening up my chest a bit. But most natural inswingers bowl pretty well chest on. The best exponent I ever saw was Bob Platt of Yorkshire, who had a stiff-legged run-up and bowled chest on. Instead of looking outside the left elbow as he delivered, he looked inside, which meant that his arm finished on the inside of his left leg instead of outside.

Of course, an outswinger becomes an inswinger to a

left-handed batsman. Jack Ikin, a very good left-hander who played for England, says that people still don't believe him when he tells them I could pitch the ball to him six inches outside his off stump and make him defend leg and middle. I always enjoyed tackling a really first-class bat like Jack because there was so much more satisfaction in getting a good player out. He played for Lancashire, of course, and the Roses matches against them were often more tense and exciting than some Tests. The Old Trafford crowd used to make me laugh, though, because if I put one round Jack Ikin's ears, or Cyril Washbrook's, they would play merry hell with me. But when I did exactly the same thing to Australian batsmen, sometimes a few hours after they had hissed and booed, they would cheer me to the echo and tell me to 'give 'em some more'! Yorkshire was always the side the other counties wanted to beat most and the general hatred directed at us—particularly from the southern teams—didn't diminish with time. We always drew bigger crowds than any other county when we travelled to play, and on the few occasions when one of the weaker counties like Somerset or Leicestershire beat us they would stand on their seats shouting and waving because Yorkshire had been humbled. You would have thought their team had scored the winning goal at Wembley, the way they went on. Even the Australians and the West Indians were scared of us. Lots of other counties boast about beating the Australians, but it's always been an Australian eleven, not their Test team. They didn't beat the full Aussie Test team like we did. All the touring sides put their strongest team against Yorkshire and when some of my team mates began to moan about this I told them to shut up and be proud—it was the biggest compliment they could pay us.

As I travelled around I also began to find out more about that invincible Yorkshire side between the wars who left us a legacy of resentment all round the country. Quite a few of the umpires and county officials had been players at that time and they told me some of the tricks they could get up to on the field. Apparently they were very good at gamesmanship and cottoned on to ideas that gave them an unfair advantage. For instance, they used to run heavily all round the wicket whilst bowling at one end and then pitch the ball into the rough patches from the other. Unfortunately some of the big men running the MCC were also playing and suffering at the hands of this side, and I swear that many Yorkshire players apart from myself were discriminated against because of the county we represented. There also seemed to be a general bias against northern players—Les Jackson of Derbyshire was only one example of a player who should have played regularly for his country. I always said that if you were a cricket genius and came from the north you might play for England, but if you were good and came from the south it was a certainty. Many players picked for England during my time just weren't good enough to make the Yorkshire side.

There was also the ludicrous business of Gentlemen and Players, before it was thankfully abolished. The Gentlemen were the amateurs and the Players were the professionals, and both Yorkshire and England strove for years to appoint an amateur captain. It was ridiculous because, apart from the many privileges they enjoyed, many of those amateurs were drawing a thousand pounds a year in expenses when we were getting paid around £750. I described them as 'shamateurs' and made myself somewhat unpopular. The snobbishness in my early days was unbelievable and I got to hate being constantly referred to as an ex-miner, as though it was something to be ashamed of. Some of those posh sods who had come straight from university into a county side and never done a real day's work in their lives used to say to me, 'I believe you are an ex-miner', with a sort of disgust in their voices. I used to snap back at them, 'What are you then—an ex-schoolboy?' because I never let anybody get away with anything when it came to a question of pride. I've often been thankful that I never had the opportunity to go to university after coming across idiots like that. My background may have been working class but I was as good a man as any of them and confident in my ability. Some of the mediocrities had no pride. If any of the MCC hierarchy happened to stroll by, they practically stood to attention, thumbs down the seams of their flannels, and there was a lot of hilarious business about who should be called 'sir'. I refused to call anybody 'sir', except the Duke of Edinburgh. I remember some cocktail parties where there were more titles than people and you would see some cricketers edging up trying to talk to 'sir' and shake hands with him. I used to ignore them and try to talk to people who had actually proved something, like Wally Hammond and Jack Hobbs. They were the real giants of the game and deserved respect.

Now I had been brought up to be honest and speak my mind and expect nothing less from other people, which is a good Yorkshire custom. But I found that some of these private conversations and remarks I had made at parties and other dos were being reported in the press, word for word. The stories that began to circulate about me, publicly and privately, astonished and enraged me. The classic and most regularly repeated one is the 'Gunga Din' incident, which probably did me more harm than any of the others. I was supposed to be sitting at the top table during a dinner given in honour of the 1952 Indian tourists by their High Commissioner when I nudged a high-ranking Indian diplomat in the ribs and said: 'Hey, Gunga Din, pass t'salt!' It is not true and is a complete mystery to me, and I hope it will now be laid to rest. The story has one fatal flaw in placing me at the top table, because they would never have seated England's most junior cap in such an exalted position. I did attend that dinner but there was no incident, and I didn't even hear the story myself until I came back from that unfortunate tour of the West Indies in 1953—which may be more than a coincidence.

Stories like that made me more than ever a prime target for the press boys who were always probing for a bit more scandal about Fred. One of them must have followed me into a night club where I was taken by a friend for a party on the eve of a Test match against New Zealand, because the next morning there was an enormous headline about me living it up at one o'clock in the morning. When I arrived at Lord's I was carpeted with a vengeance, which made me boil when I thought about the things the golden boys had got away with time and again. There was only one way to answer the charges, and I did it—I took six wickets and helped to put New Zealand out just after lunch.

By this time I had changed my sleeping habits. I found that getting up at half past five or six o'clock in the morning, which I had done ever since I'd been a newspaper delivery boy, was no use. By the time a match started at 11.30 a.m. I was half knackered, so I found it a positive advantage to go to bed late and get up late. Being up at one o'clock in the morning just before a match wasn't really unusual.

Unfortunately there was another spot of bother in a night club round about the same time when an Irishman and a coloured chap asked if they could share my table. I readily agreed, but became very annoyed with them when the cabaret started—it was the first time I had seen Danny La Rue, then almost unknown. They started yapping away so I told them both to shut up until the show was over. At this the Irishman took a swing at me so I hit him—hard. Then the coloured man rushed at me, but four waiters jumped in between us and kept us apart. When one of them called me 'Mr Trueman' this man peered at me and said, 'Good God! It's not Freddie Trueman, is it? I'm from Jamaica and I'm your greatest fan out there!' So we shook hands, split a bottle of champagne and talked cricket whilst the Irishman still lay on the floor unconscious.

At least I was actually there when that fracas happened. As far as most of the stories in circulation about me were concerned, I was in another place at the time, but most people didn't want to believe it. The most blatant case of this kind concerned an hotel in Bristol which made an official complaint about me to the Yorkshire Committee and I was hauled before them to explain my 'bad language and disgusting behaviour' whilst staying there during a match against Gloucester. The hotel management demanded a full apology or Freddie Trueman would never be allowed to darken their doors again. That was one of the rare occasions when I had a complete answer. I sat in front of that committee and waited patiently, whilst they waffled on about the dreadful charges laid against me, until they allowed me to speak.

So I said: 'Well, if it wasn't for the set-up which exists at the Yorkshire County Cricket Club I wouldn't be sitting here today.' Whereupon Sir William Worsley, president of Yorkshire, who was a real gentleman and one of the few on the committee who liked me, asked me what on earth I meant by that remark. I went on to tell him that even the amazing Freddie Trueman couldn't play for Yorkshire at Bristol and for England at Lord's on one and the same day. And if someone had taken the trouble to look up the fixture list this pantomime could have been avoided. I had left the Yorkshire team at Taunton the day they moved up to Bristol, and I had travelled to London to practise in the nets with the rest of the England team. Sir William grabbed the fixture list and checked up. Then he blew his top, demanding to know what the devil I was doing in front of the committee and who was responsible. He also said the hotel must withdraw its complaint and make a full apology to me forthwith. I wanted to take the letter to my solicitor and sue them out of sight, but eventually it was smoothed over.

There was another row when the manageress of an hotel in Worksop wrote to Yorkshire County Cricket Club to say that Freddie Trueman would be barred from ever entering her establishment again because of his disgraceful behaviour. I had never stayed at that place in my life, so when I passed by in my car a few weeks later I walked into that hotel, went straight to the bar to order a gin and tonic and waited for any reaction. A woman served me and I asked her if she was the manageress. She said she was, so I asked her if she knew who I was—and she didn't. I said I found that fact strange because she had barred me from ever entering the place again, and she said she didn't understand. Then a barman standing near by said, 'That's Freddie Trueman'. She just didn't know where to look, so after a few well-chosen words I walked out, leaving the drink untouched and unpaid for on the bar.

The Yorkshire team had, in fact, made something of a fuss there when they stayed overnight because they hadn't been able to play dominoes, but I hadn't been with them. You could be sure that if ever my team mates got mixed up in a spot of bother, then I would be blamed for it, even if I was two hundred miles away at the time. And it went on for years. Perhaps on occasion it was a genuine, if inexcusable, mistake because one of the Yorkshire players did look a bit like me, but I know it was mainly a direct result of the 'terrible Trueman' tag pinned on me by my critics and the gossips.

Yet another incident centred on an hotel blew up when a Yorkshire member reported me to the committee for being in the Queen's Hotel, Leeds, at 2.30 a.m. in the middle of a match. He also said I was drunk and in the company of two women and had roared off in a car whilst clearly unfit to drive. By this time the committee had learned to check the facts and the club secretary delivered a severe rebuke because I was playing in Brighton at the time. Yet that man was a member, a keen supporter of Yorkshire and was convinced it was me. I am convinced that there were one or two—or maybe more—men who looked a bit like me and pretended they were me. I once actually met one, and he was driving a taxi at the time. When he looked at me he said, 'It's not Freddie Trueman, is it? By hell, you did me a great favour once. I used to go round in a baker's van trying to sell cakes and one day I called at an hotel looking for business. Well, they looked at me and said, "Blimey—it's Freddie Trueman! How are you? Marvellous to see you—what are you selling?"' I asked this man if he had put them right and he said, 'Hell, no! I got a bloody great order from

1   The house where I was born, years later. It's now demolished

2   My Dad in about 1938

3 During National Service in the RAF, 1952

4 Showing our kid brother Dennis (the Menace)
what it's all about. About 1953

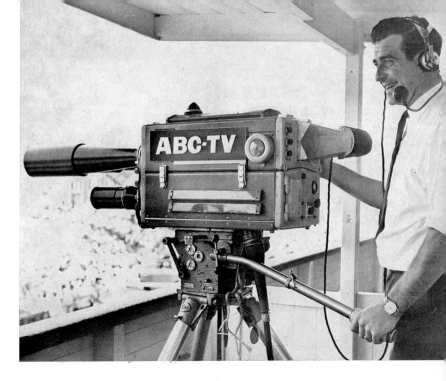

5 Trying my hand as cameraman, Headingley in the 1950s

6 In the West Indies, 1953

7 Wound up and ready to deliver

8 One of my favourite pictures of me in action, 1956

them every week for three years because they thought I was you.'

The curious thing was that, although he was dark and thickset, he really didn't look anything like me and admitted it. Anyway, that was funny—he profited and no one got hurt. But there were occasions too numerous to count when other people created serious problems for me. My first wife, Enid, whom I met and married in Scarborough in 1955, used to go off her head with the stories she heard. Once a person went to the trouble of ringing her up to say I had definitely been seen picking up a model outside a big fashion shop in Scarborough at 5.30 p.m. That day I had been playing cricket in London until 7 p.m. Another time, when we were living in York, I rang Enid at night to find her in a terribly upset state. She had met a man in the street who told her he had just seen me at a beer cellar in York with a German girl. And she seemed to believe it. I told her it was impossible because I was speaking to her from London and gave her my phone number to ring back if she doubted me.

What made all these stories even more stupid was the fact that throughout my career I was one of the most sober men in county cricket. Yet the public believed I was a real boozer and I became extremely irritated by continually meeting up with people I'd never seen before to hear them say that the last time we met we'd got drunk together. And there were even more who said they understood I was a regular at their father's pub or their uncle's pub and wasn't I a bit of a lad, eh! Accompanied by a nudge in the ribs and a wink. Who the hell all these people were that were going round pretending to be me I don't know, but they were obviously having one whale of a time.

Apart from taking holy orders and entering a monastery, I could think of no effective way of stopping all this rubbish. In fact, I did act like a monk on many occasions —avoiding crowds, even going my own way on tour with the Yorkshire and England teams. When they were out on the town I would slope off and eat a quiet steak somewhere. Many's the time I went to bed at nine o'clock at night after a match, absolutely knackered. At my peak I was bowling more than a thousand overs a season for Yorkshire alone, which is unheard of for a man of my pace. But I was a folk hero, conspicuous by my absence from the rest of the team. Everyone assumed I was attending an even bigger orgy somewhere else and when they went to look for me never thought of checking my room. God alone knows what was being said about me, but in some hotels the chambermaids refused to bring breakfast to my room! Managements were always embarrassed and said they could think of no reason for their refusal to enter a room alone with me, so I can only assume they had been listening to some of the ludicrous stories in circulation and thought they were going to be raped for sure.

We were still winning nothing at Yorkshire because the dressing-room remained as divided and bitchy as ever. Norman Yardley held on to the captaincy even after Len Hutton became skipper of England. It must have been galling for Len having to take orders from someone else at county level when he was boss of the national team and I'm sure he badly wanted to be captain of Yorkshire as well. I was also certain that Norman had no intention of allowing that to happen. As it turned out, Norman didn't announce his retirement until just after Len had announced his. Norman was an amateur, which was supposed to help you to be a captain, and he certainly knew about tactics and how to read a game. He was also good to me, being helpful and friendly and not bowling me into the ground like some skippers did. But in my opinion Norman wasn't the strong man that Yorkshire needed at the helm in those days and he let people like Johnny Wardle and Bob Appleyard get away with far too much. They wanted to bowl all the time and seemed to be able to talk him out of making a change even when it was clear to everyone that one was required.

When Norman retired in 1955, Billy Sutcliffe took over, and what happened to him was really a disgrace to Yorkshire cricket. He was a very likeable man and a superb bat—good enough to have walked into the England team had he been playing today. I fell out with the Yorkshire crowd during Billy's captaincy. He was the son of the legendary Herbert Sutcliffe, who made more than 150 centuries, and they were on to him all the time, shouting insults like 'You'll never be as good as your father, Sutcliffe!' In many ways I'm glad my own son doesn't look as though he is going to be a cricketer, because it must be hell to follow a famous father. Billy also failed to master Johnny Wardle and eventually a group of players got a petition together demanding his resignation. I refused to have anything to do with it, but Billy decided to pack it in after that. It must have broken his heart.

And then came the era of Ronnie Burnet. He was the captain of the second eleven at the time and an amateur —but an honest one, who only claimed his genuine expenses. Now Ronnie would probably be the first to admit that he wasn't county standard and when he was appointed Yorkshire's captain in 1958 he was thirty-nine and had never played for the senior team. But he was a

natural leader. I played under him for the first time after
I had missed two matches with a badly blistered left foot.
Just after it healed I noticed there was a second team
fixture at Middlesbrough so I suggested it would be a
good opportunity to try it out in a match which didn't
matter. By an odd coincidence, Bob Appleyard was also
making a comeback after injury in that match and Brian
Close was in the team too. He had been having a bad
time and was trying to play himself back into form. Right
from the start, Ronnie showed what he was made of. He
ordered Brian Close to open the batting and when Brian
objected told him he would either go in first or go back
home. Brian climbed down, and I thought to myself that
Ronnie hadn't made a bad start at all. When our innings
was finished he came to me and told me to bowl only
four or five overs to start with to see how the injured foot
stood up to it. I did as I was told, but when Bob Appleyard came on to bowl I began to wonder what would
happen when Ronnie tried to take him off and he wanted
to keep bowling. Eventually Ronnie said, 'Okay, Bob—
put your sweater on.' As I expected, Bob told him he
didn't want to come off and Ronnie asked him again to
take his sweater. Again Bob protested, so Ronnie commanded, 'Put your sweater on and do as you are told!'
and walked away, leaving Bob completely nonplussed.
It was then that I thought that Ronnie Burnet would do
for me and I supported him right from the start, although
I knew we would have to do a bit of carrying.

Clearly he got the job not for his cricketing prowess
but to forge Yorkshire into a united team, which they
hadn't been since I joined in 1949. It took guts for a second
team man to march into our dressing-room and start
disciplining the established stars and England players,
and he did it. But not without casualties. I suppose no

one resented Ronnie's appointment more than Johnny Wardle. I'm sure Johnny thought the job was bound to be his because of his experience, knowledge and length of service and he would probably have made a good captain, although I considered he had too severe an attitude to younger players and expected too much from them too soon. He must also have been keen to claim the honour of becoming Yorkshire's first professional skipper. The bitter disappointment he felt could only have been made worse by the treatment he had received from the MCC selectors. In my opinion Johnny was the finest slow left arm bowler of my time, but he was denied a regular place in the Test side. Poor Johnny must have thought he was missing out on everything.

With him you had two bowlers in one, because when the conditions were right he could bowl his funny stuff—Chinamen and googlies—out of the back of his hand and beat anybody. And he could bat. Not many people realize that Johnny took a hundred wickets in Test cricket, a lot of them on the South African tour of 1956 when his performance was so brilliant that a lot of people thought he might displace Tony Lock. But he was overlooked like so many Yorkshire players before and after him.

Naturally the situation in the Yorkshire dressing-room was a bit tense when Ronnie took over. This placed me in a difficult situation because I was very friendly with both him and Johnny, so I kept quiet and got out of the way quickly if I saw trouble brewing. It couldn't last, of course, and the whole thing blew up in Ronnie's first season when we went to play Lancashire at Old Trafford. Apparently Johnny had informed the committee that he had written a series of articles for the *Daily Mail* which criticized some people, including the new captain. We were getting ready for the match when Ronnie marched in, shut the door and said: 'Right, lads, you may read some articles in the paper written by Johnny Wardle which will probably bring the other press lads and the radio people round here later today. You are to keep your mouths shut. As for Johnny Wardle, I've just sent him packing. He's finished with Yorkshire for good!'

We just sat there stunned, unbelieving. None of us had expected this, and I still think it a great shame for such a magnificent cricketer to go out in public disgrace. He had served Yorkshire well for years and carried the county's attack on his shoulders during the time I was in the RAF and Bob Appleyard was in and out with injuries. Nor was it necessary for Yorkshire to be so vindictive when Johnny looked round for another job. They warned off other counties who were offering him terms and he wound up playing on Saturdays in the Lancashire league.

Yorkshire didn't do too well in the county championship in 1958, but it was hardly surprising. We had only three of the old team left. But the sacrifice certainly worked out well for the county, as Ronnie brought on youngsters like Don Wilson, Philip Sharpe, Brian Bolus and Jackie Birkinshaw. He created a tremendous team spirit and was responsible for laying the foundation of the decade of success which was to follow. We even won the championship in 1959, but some of the edge was taken off that triumph when the committee gave us a bonus of £50, which worked out at £2 a match before tax. Not enough to pay the electricity bill for a quarter! Then we received a roasting from the committee for being insubordinate and not writing to thank them for their generous gift (which was exactly the same as that paid to the championship team of 1932). Because he was an amateur,

Ronnie Burnet wasn't allowed to receive money, so he was told to select a gift to commemorate the occasion— but it mustn't exceed the sum of £20! It was typical of Yorkshire's miserable treatment of their players, which never changed as long as I played for them.

Chapter 5

Disaster in Australia

I don't believe the MCC selectors ever wanted to pick me to play for England. Public opinion forced their hand. In 1953, just after I had routed the Indians, they gave me only one match against the Australian tourists—the vital one, for the Ashes. And when they came to choose the tour side to go to Australia in 1954 I was top of the English averages with 144 wickets, the most successful bowler in the land. I was also the only fast bowler with well over a hundred wickets, because Frank Tyson had only 67, Brian Statham and Peter Loader about 80 each and Trevor Bailey around a hundred. They all went. So did Alec Bedser, and he was just going on a sentimental trip because he was too old for that class of cricket.

I knew before the team was announced that I wouldn't be included. Players are asked well in advance if they are available for selection and I hadn't been asked. When the news was released all hell broke loose in the news-papers, particularly in Yorkshire, about my exclusion. This was climaxed by the sensational story in the *Sunday People*—for which I now write—which claimed they knew three players who had said they would refuse to go to Australia if I was chosen. They didn't name them. There was a Yorkshire committee meeting at Harrogate to consider suing the *Sunday People*—which I should have done independently, of course, but I was too inexperienced in those days and had no one to advise me. Tom Taylor, the president of Yorkshire at the time, who had played as an amateur in the 1890s, persuaded them to drop the matter and then an extraordinary thing happened. John Nash, the county secretary, came to me and said that the MCC had in fact asked if I was available but he had forgotten to tell me! It seemed to me a cover-up job, because he hadn't forgotten to tell Len Hutton and Johnny Wardle.

The kind of person dominating cricket throughout most of my career came from a wealthy family, played cricket for his university and then a county without ever proving much. The game was full of people like this, relics from the Victorian era. They had no idea about the modern game, and we would have won a lot more Tests without them. Some of them had won England caps as amateurs in the thirties, and from what I hear wouldn't have made the Yorkshire second team if they had been professionals. They looked down on the man who made his living from the game, and considered an amateur, particularly if he had a cricket blue at Oxford or Cambridge, a much superior choice for the England team.

I once heard a story from an old professional cricketer, now dead, called Jim Sims, who played for England against Australia in 1936. Jim started life as a miner but was so good at cricket that they took him on the Lord's ground staff. In those days Lord's would send their ground staff to play for various teams all over the place, instructing them to seek out the captains and report— and remember to call them 'sir'. Well, Jim used to march up to captains, stand to attention and say, 'Sims, sir. Lord's ground staff', and was nearly always sent in at around No. 10 and only got a chance to bowl occasionally. This went on for a long time and Jim got fed up. One day he changed his tactics, strolled up to the captain and said: 'Morning, sir. My name is Morton Sims, from Lord's.' And the captain replied, 'Good man! Would you like to open the batting?'

Now I'm not trying to stir up any North versus South prejudice, because I think that divisions like that are both stupid and harmful, but there was no doubt in my mind that the MCC would pick a southerner if possible, a northerner only if pushed, and a Yorkshireman only when they couldn't possibly avoid it. I often thought the point would have been proved if the Australians and other touring sides had played five Tests against the South and another five against the North, because the full England side always carried passengers. Many's the time I've lost my temper on tour and said to an England skipper: 'What the hell have you picked that mug for—he's not good enough to play for England,' and they have actually replied: 'No, but he's a nice chap and he had a jolly good season with his county.'

A northern player could burst through the barrier like I did—by first of all playing so well that they couldn't ignore me and then by shouting and creating a fuss when I was unfairly treated. I had to shout because I realized that it was the only way I was going to get my talent recognized. Knocking wickets down right, left and centre and picking up a lot of catches obviously wasn't going to be enough. Muhammad Ali was forced to do exactly the same thing, but I was ten years and more ahead of him. I also knew how to 'psyche' an opponent before he had the strength to knock his teddy bear over.

To make this approach work I'm afraid I had to turn myself into something I didn't really want to be. I know I'm an extrovert by nature, but on the cricket field I became an arrogant bastard. I used every device I could think of—shouting, growling, glaring, anything to make an impact. Every time I came up against a batsman with a big reputation I would go after him with every ounce of strength in my body, and use every psychological weapon in the book to try to frighten him into submission. Some thought I had a personal grudge against them and resented me, but I was only using them to prove a point to the selectors.

I calculate that I missed at least thirty Tests because the MCC never stopped looking for an excuse to drop me. Other Yorkshire players had an even worse deal. Brian Close, the best left-handed bat of his generation, should have played in about seventy Tests but got picked for less than a third of that number. Some of the players who displaced him weren't good enough to clean his boots—and he was a brilliant captain and a better bowler than most. Johnny Wardle I've mentioned already, but perhaps the worst injustice of all was done to Jimmy Binks, the greatest uncapped wicket keeper who ever played cricket. After Godfrey Evans, he was far and away the best in the country but they picked anybody but him—Roy Swetman of Surrey, Geoff Millman of Notts, Jim Parks of Sussex. Nor would I ever have picked Alan Moss, John Dews and John Warr, all of Middlesex, or Brian Taylor of Essex, or Bob Barber and Alan Smith, or Dick Richardson of Worcester or Alan Oakman of Sussex. Now Alan is another pal of mine who used to open the batting for Sussex and he was chosen to go to South Africa in 1956 after scoring about sixteen hundred runs from sixty knocks or so. I was a bowler going in ninth or tenth for Yorkshire and I had scored nine hundred runs from thirty knocks! It was ridiculous.

They only let me go on four tours—twice to the West

Indies (1953–4 and 1959–60) and twice to Australia (1958–9 and 1962–3). Never once was I picked for the cream and jelly trips to India, Pakistan and South Africa, which cost me a lot of Test wickets. In fact, I only ever played four times against Pakistan (and got 22 wickets), six times against South Africa (27 wickets) and nine against India (53 wickets, no less), compared to nineteen matches against Australia and eighteen against the West Indians. Peter May came to me when I had been excluded from one tour to South Africa to say how sorry he was that I wasn't going. But he assured me that I would play for England again because he had told the selectors that he wanted the best side next time and it couldn't be that without me. It wasn't much comfort at the time.

All through 1955 and 1956 I hovered about the Test match scene getting the odd match against the South Africans and the Australians, but only when injuries practically left them with no choice bar the recall of Harold Larwood from the old folks' home. Incidentally I was becoming heartily sick of hearing the name of Harold Larwood because the sherry and old school tie brigade were for ever comparing me with him, usually unfavourably. My reprieve came in 1957 when I was recalled to play against the touring West Indians, and I didn't waste the chance. I got 22 Test wickets, another 15 against the New Zealanders and bowled myself straight on to the boat to Australia in 1958.

What a complete, bloody disaster that tour turned out to be. We went out, supposedly the strongest team ever to leave these shores (although I would have made a few changes), and the holders of the Ashes. Peter May led the side, and though he was the best amateur skipper I ever played under, he was no Len Hutton. But we had

Freddie Brown as the tour manager, a vital job, and I considered him both unsuitable and ill-mannered. An amateur and ex-captain of the MCC, he made it clear from the start that he did not like me—in fact, before we even left England he was threatening to send me home if I caused any trouble.

In 1958 Australian cricket was in a hell of a state. It was the time of the great throwing controversy involving Meckiff and Rorke—and others. Our management in their wisdom decided to go and see Don Bradman, most famous Aussie cricketer of all time, to complain about Meckiff and Rorke and ask that they be prevented from using their unfair action. I told the deputation they were wasting their time because we hadn't a leg to stand on. Don Bradman would just turn round and ask them what they intended to do about the doubtful action of Lock and Loader. For my effrontery I was told to shut my mouth because I didn't know what I was talking about, though I had ten years' experience as a fast bowler and knew a thing or two about a fast bowler's action. They went off to see the great man and he promptly told them to put their own house in order, just as I forecast. But they weren't big enough to come back and admit I was right. I considered that Meckiff's action was totally illegal and that he should never have been allowed to play. In a book of his he described me as a thrower, which demonstrated how much he knew about the game. Even my worst critics on the MCC had to admit that my action was beyond criticism.

So there we were, both teams chucking the ball at each other, and just to make it a bigger shambles their umpires stuffed us out of sight. They started no-balling me—of all people—and we just couldn't get favourable decisions. In one Test there were two incidents which are

77

hilarious at this distance, but then they amazed and infuriated all of us. To begin with, Frank Tyson hit Jimmy Burke smack on the glove and Godfrey Evans, playing with a broken finger, took off in a dive to catch the ball between first and second slip, taking the skin off his arm in the process. It was one of the greatest catches I've ever seen by a wicket keeper. Jimmy Burke stood there, shaking his arm in pain—and the umpire gave him not out! Frank was so livid he gave him a bouncer next ball and hit him in the nose. A bit later Colin Macdonald was run out by at least five yards but the umpire had gone to the wrong side of the wicket and turned down the appeal. Even the Aussies were so embarrassed by this time that Colin Macdonald came up to me and said: 'For Christ's sake, Fred, bowl me one straight. I'm fed up with this.' So I bowled one straight, he just had a swing at it and his stumps were flattened. That must be the easiest Test wicket I've ever taken!

Right from the moment we landed in Australia I took some gruelling punishment because I was appointed the team's workhorse and made to bowl nearly all the time. Some of the people we took on that tour just weren't strong enough to face up to a six-month tour in that heat on top of a five-month county season. All the way to Brisbane I sweated, and then I developed a mysterious back illness which kept me out of the first Test. What brought it on was never really known, but it hit me on both my tours to Australia when I got to Brisbane. I had X-rays and painkilling injections and specialists examined me without much improvement. And then Freddie Brown came to me and said that if I wasn't going to be fit, I might as well go back home, which hurt more than the backache. Willie Watson had slipped and hurt his leg on the way out, been flown on from Ceylon to Australia for an operation and hadn't played a match until we arrived in Brisbane, but no one suggested he should go home. I went and complained about Brown to Peter May. He didn't say much but went to see the manager and I heard nothing more about it. The trouble cleared up when we went to Adelaide, but it had nothing to do with all the doctors and surgeons who had messed about with me. I met an old lady in Adelaide who told me to kick the medics into touch, go out into the garden and fill a bag full of lemons fresh from the tree. Then I was to squeeze them into a glass, add the same amount of water and drink it first thing in the morning before I had even cleaned my teeth. I was ready to try anything, and hobbled away to the nearest lemon tree. Three days later I was bowling again. People laugh when I tell them that story, but I'm convinced those lemons did the trick. In fact, I was so fit by the next match that I got nine wickets, took a couple of catches and scored fifty with the bat. I thought I was certain to play in the second Test but I was wrong, and we lost. That put us two down in the rubber. They brought me back to help try to pull us back out of the mess for the third Test, but the match was drawn and we went back to Adelaide knowing that if we didn't win the next two the Ashes would ·be back again with the Aussies.

The Adelaide Test turned out to be a travesty. I had a row with an umpire who was no-balling me for my front foot being just over the front line—although he seemed to be allowing Gordon Rorke to bowl from sixteen yards! I collected a 'pair' with the bat, but the decision against me in the second innings was typical of the umpiring we had to suffer on that tour. I was batting against Richie Benaud and intended to try to knock him out of the ground if he pitched one up to me. He did just that, but

I was so eager to get at it that I hit the ground with my bat and it bounced into the air. All I could do was watch the ball come through and just miss my off stump. My bat was two feet away from the ball. Wally Grout, the Aussie wicket keeper, caught it, whipped off my bails and appealed for a stumping. The square leg umpire said 'Not out', but his partner at the other end gave me out caught behind the wicket!

There was no way we were going to win that match and we finished the series getting thumped four-nil, with one drawn. You can imagine what was being said about us back home. But I did my best and considered that I emerged with my honour intact. At least I had another twenty Test wickets to add to the total despite only playing in three of the five Tests. I also got a sackful of wickets in State and one-day matches because they never stopped bowling me as if I was a bloody machine. I even had to do twelfth man duties in one minor match, with a Test match just coming up and two of the other pace bowlers injured. Godfrey Evans was very angry about this, pointing out that I was the only fit fast bowler in the party and needed to be rested. But they wouldn't listen—they never did.

I was warned at the start of that trip that my aggressive nature would get me into trouble with Aussie spectators, particularly the notorious 'Hill' at Sydney which could make the Stretford End at Manchester United look like a meeting of the Band of Hope. But I found a lot in common with the Australians, players and spectators alike. I liked their basic attitude. The players were good shouters, perhaps a bit too cocky when they were winning. But you had to watch them when they were losing —they hated losing. I found that the only way to deal with an Aussie cricketer was to get stuck in—like they always did with us—and then you found that underneath all the noise was a good bloke. I made many friends over there—indeed, Norm O'Neill of New South Wales was to become one of my best pals. Their supporters had exactly the same frame of mind. They respected and admired a man who would give as much as he took without squealing. When I came up against the Hill during the Sydney Test they baited me a bit, so I threw a few wisecracks right back at them, informing them that their ancestors came from the best jails in Britain amongst other things. They loved it. Like the West Indians, the Aussie crowds really enjoy their cricket and they become intent on having a damn good day out, bringing plenty of beer with them. It was hot during that match at Sydney and when I was fielding on the boundary between overs one of the jokers held up a can of Fosters and shouted: 'Hey, Fred—how would you like a beer?' I shouted back that I could kill one, and when I went up to the wicket for another over asked Peter May if I could take the man up on the offer, just for a bit of a laugh. Peter realized it would be good public relations and agreed, so long as I only had a sip. When I went to the boundary again the man called out again so I thanked him, grabbed the can and took a quick swallow. The entire Hill clapped and cheered and when I returned after the next over there were cans of ale lined up waiting for me all round the fence. From then on I was in with the Hill and they were great to me.

Generally speaking, I got along splendidly with everyone on tours overseas, umpires excepted. The following winter I was selected to go on the 1959–60 tour to the West Indies, scene of my so-called disgrace six years before. I was careful to avoid trouble this time, although

I did have a row on the ship taking us out there—with the captain, I'm afraid. It turned out to be a good and happy tour, partly because Walter Robins was appointed manager. Walter was the only MCC mandarin I ever really liked and got along with. He had a sense of humour and knew how to handle cricketers when the difficult situations arose, as they always do on trips like that. Seeing the same sixteen or seventeen faces every day at breakfast, lunch and dinner, and then at the inevitable cocktail party afterwards, can be very irritating. And it gets worse towards the end of a tour. Usually it's hot, wives and families are being missed and there's always at least one player consistently failing where it matters most—on the cricket field. Tempers crack, things are said which aren't really meant and you can find yourself in the middle of a polite, travelling brawl unless somebody has the courage and intelligence to spot problems early and deal with them. Walter Robins was pretty good at that, which made a welcome change.

For me it was probably the best tour of the lot. I bowled on top form and we won the series, even though Peter May became ill and had to hand over the captaincy to Colin Cowdrey. I'm afraid my opinion of Colin as a skipper didn't amount to much, although he was a batsman of the highest order.

We had the usual upsets with the West Indian umpires. A strange breed of animal, umpires. In Britain we have the finest in the world because they are practically full-time professionals. In Australia I found they could go either way, in India they were terrible—I remember once in Bombay on an exhibition tour putting a man out four times before he actually went back to the pavilion— but in the West Indies they have the worst in the world. For example, in one match I managed to find a wet spot and made the ball rear up. It hit one batsman a real crack on his glove and the catch was taken at short leg. But the umpire turned the appeal down and when I protested said the ball had struck his thigh pad. I told him that you don't normally find a thigh pad in front of a man's throat and pointed to the batsman, who had taken off his glove to inspect the damage to his hand. Now even an Aussie will often stand if the edge was just a thin tickle in the hope of a not out decision, but to remain whatever the umpire says when you know you are out breaks all the unwritten laws of cricket. This man was being so blasé into the bargain that I was really furious and I'm afraid I hit him in the mouth with the next ball and he had to be carried off. Colin Cowdrey got very worried about that but I thought it was poetic justice.

Although cowardice is no excuse, I did feel a little sorry for the West Indian umpires because they were sometimes in danger from the crowds. Sadly that tour will be chiefly remembered for the riot in Trinidad. Now the West Indians are marvellous cricket enthusiasts. It's their national game, they are very knowledgeable about it and when they pay to see a match they expect a full day's entertainment and a bit of excitement. They also go to meet up with their mates, have a few beers, a few bets and probably the odd scrap, all fitted round the cricket. They came to the Trinidad Test in their thousands—they were even hanging out of the trees. They don't care overmuch for umpires in Trinidad and on the third day the crowd definitely turned ugly. You can always depend on a bottle or two bouncing around the outfield when their team are losing—which they certainly were—but that day it began to rain glass. Then they poured on to the pitch and I thought I was going to have to fight for my life until they called out, 'Don't worry, Fred—we're not going to touch you. We want the umpires.' All the players got off the field as calmly as they could and the police moved in to rescue the umpires. Even with a slice taken out of the middle of the match, we still thrashed them with time to spare.

Once again I deposited more sweat in the dust than anyone else. I lost more than a stone in weight. Only Ray Illingworth, an off-spinner, bowled more overs than me, but I took the most wickets overall and the twenty-one I took in the Tests set a record for an English bowler in the West Indies. That put my Test total up to 149 wickets, and I was immensely pleased with myself because it meant I'd passed Hedley Verity's total of 137. Now Verity was a name constantly mentioned in the pavilion at Headingley as one of the greatest Yorkshire bowlers of all time. So when I got back home I mentioned the fact that I'd overhauled him during a chat with one of the members of the Yorkshire Committee.

'Maybe,' said this man. 'But you must realize you are playing more Tests than Hedley Verity.' I pointed out that he was wrong—Verity had played five or six more Tests than me at that stage, but he wouldn't have it. It was worse than arguing with a brick wall. Even though I had 149 Test wickets, and had done more than my share to make Yorkshire the top county again, they wouldn't admit I was as good as the old timers. Or even a really class bowler. The men who ran Yorkshire could make you feel miserable even when you were beating the world.

Chapter 6

Breakdown of a Marriage

If things were going better for me on the cricket field at the end of the fifties, they certainly weren't at home. In fact, my marriage was beginning to break up. On reflection, I suppose it was inevitable.

I met Enid in 1951 at a cocktail party given by her father, who was the Mayor of Scarborough at the time. She was a very beautiful girl and I was smitten by her. We kept in touch when I did my National Service, married in 1955 and set up house in West Ayton outside Scarborough. The first five years or so passed by happily, although there wasn't much common ground between us. She loved dancing and was very good at it, but I had no interest at all in going out at night pounding round a dance floor. On the other hand, I felt that she didn't take the slightest interest in cricket from start to finish.

I worked hard at trying to make the marriage a good one. I believed in family life and had been raised to regard marriage as a contract for life. I wanted a home to be proud of and spent my money on buying decent furniture and keeping a good table. Nothing went on gambling, which I have always considered a waste of time. If I had a weakness, it was for flash sports cars— but I needed fast transport. Living in Scarborough made life very difficult for me as a husband and father even when I was playing in Yorkshire. For instance, Sheffield is a hundred miles away from Scarborough and that meant a two and a half hour drive in those days. I would leave home at eight o'clock in the morning to make sure of getting to Sheffield, Leeds or Bradford, Yorkshire's principal home grounds, by 10.30. Then I would bowl fast all day until the evening and drive all the way back, often arriving just in time to go to bed. It wasn't much of a life but I did it willingly in the interests of marital happiness. But how I managed to drive for five hours and bowl between twenty and thirty overs flat out all in the same day for year after year will remain a mystery for all time. Sometimes I feel I ought to leave my body to medical science so they can have a good look at the way it was put together.

There was nothing I could do about being away from home when we travelled to play other counties. And the six-month tours abroad placed a tremendous strain on our relationship. I'm astonished that many more divorces don't occur among the members of the England cricket team, because there is no way you can be a husband and father at a distance of five or twelve thousand miles, speaking occasionally on the telephone.

Most people think it very glamorous to spend the English winter on the other side of the world, basking in the sunshine. But bowling fast in those temperatures and humidities is harder than working down a pit and many's the time I've sat in an empty hotel bedroom in Australia or the Caribbean trying to make the air conditioning work and wondering what the hell was going on back home, and wishing I was sitting in front of a log fire in Scarborough with a pint of ale in my hand. Christmas was the really bad time to be away and I think it would make sense if tours were suspended for two weeks so that the team could go home to their families. Perhaps there will come a time when the Cricket Board of Control will pay for wives to be flown out after a reasonable time, to accompany the team for the rest of the tour. Until that day dawns my advice to any young cricketer is to steer clear of marriage until his international career is over. If I had my time again I certainly would.

Cricketers are human, and when you are used to a healthy marital relationship it's more than flesh and blood can stand to go without sex for six whole months. Not that opportunity didn't exist—indeed it was thrust at us from all sides most of the time. There were rich and good-looking women chasing us around day and night. I suppose it's the same at the top level in any sport, but it certainly amazed me when I first met it. Of course, the amateurs didn't need to be subjected to the same pressures. They were allowed to bring their wives on tour if they wanted to, a privilege denied the professionals. They paid all the bills, or so it was said.

Enid never accused me of sleeping with other women on the tours, but she was an intelligent woman and must have known that I had the odd bird. There were plenty of things which upset her, but that wasn't one. She understandably got mad at not being able to live a reasonable life with me, even when I was home. The phone would never stop ringing and people were for ever dropping round to see me—me, not her. Often she wouldn't be included on the invitation to parties and functions, and at one stage I refused to go anywhere unless she was officially included. Even when she was, people would totally ignore her and talk just to me or try to drag me off to meet someone else. I used to try to force her into the conversation, but it rarely worked. No red-blooded woman is going to stand for that on top of all the separations, so the rows started.

There were always people around when we needed to be on our own. A classic example happened when I returned home once from Birmingham having broken another record whilst bowling out the West Indians. Enid came to meet me, full of affection and happiness for me and expecting just the two of us to be there. When she arrived she could scarcely get to me for the press and crowds of well wishers. She lost her temper in front of everybody, shouting, 'One day you'll come home without your bloody friends all hanging on your back!' and left. I was upset and disappointed at the time, but I can understand now just how fed up she must have felt.

And there was the celebrated occasion when the BBC made a programme about my life, invited Enid to take part—and she had a right go at me, in front of several million people. She spelt out how impossible it was to have any home life married to Freddie Trueman. I can't say I liked it, but I don't hold it against her. It would have taken an angel to enjoy being my wife at that time.

The rows and scenes got worse and worse until I frequently left the house and spent the night in my car. There was one notable occasion in 1961 when I was playing against the Australians at Headingley, and on the Saturday afternoon I had a six wickets for one run spell in less than an hour to put them all out. The press were calling it the finest piece of pace bowling ever seen in a Test and I sat there after the match, smoking my pipe and drinking a cup of tea, with queues of people interviewing me, taking my photograph, patting me on the back, asking for my autograph. And I wondered to myself what they would have thought if they had known I'd spent the previous night in the back of my car in a Leeds car park with an overcoat for a blanket, arriving at the ground before anyone else so that I could have a wash and a shave. There had been another row.

For a long time my address was often The Car, Yorkshire Dales, and by 1964 I had taken enough. I walked out intending that it would be final and stayed in an hotel near Skipton. But one day when I went back to the house to see Karen, our daughter, I looked at Enid and knew straight away that she was pregnant. I kept quiet and waited. Eventually she said, 'I've got something to tell you', but I told her she needn't bother because I knew what it was. I went straight back to her, and she gave birth to our twins. I did my best—bought another, bigger house in Scarborough and tried hard to make life a bit happier. It didn't work for long. I stuck it for another six years, often having to go away to the Dales for a few days for some peace, and then we both admitted that there was nothing to gain by living together.

I made the break again, this time for good. But it wasn't easy. Night after night I sat alone in hotels and friends' houses and cried like a kid. I was convinced that my life was as good as finished. I had very few friends to turn to because I'd spent years building a wall round myself to keep people out. I was a genuine loner, and basically still am. By that time I had retired from cricket so I didn't even have that to fill my time and thoughts. It was a desperate period, the worst crisis of my life. To begin with, I just didn't believe in divorce. But the thing that really cut me in two was parting from my children, and wondering what they would think of me when they grew up. I had respected my father to the end of his life, and I wanted their respect.

Children have always got through to me, and my own are more important than anything else you can name.

There is one side to me which I normally keep quiet about, but if you want the full picture of Freddie Trueman you should know that I work hard for children's charities whenever I get the chance. It started years ago when I was a youngster trying to make the grade in the Yorkshire team. Maurice Leyland, to whom I shall always be grateful, was full of ideas to encourage my career and made a habit of striking small bets with me. He thought I should get a lot more runs with the bat and started by wagering a pint that I wouldn't score a half-century one season. I won that, and the following year he bet a pound of tobacco and a pint that I couldn't score another fifty and take ten wickets in a match. I won again. Next time he bet a stone of humbugs I wouldn't get a half-century and six wickets in one innings, both in the same match. The first game we played at Bradford that season was against Hampshire, and I took six wickets very cheaply which left us chasing 114 for the bonus points. Johnny Wardle was acting captain that day and he sent me in at No. 4 to have a belt. We needed 52 runs, and I scored them all. Maurice came with a stone of humbugs to the next match, which was at Harrogate. The press had got to know about the bet and worked up a story about it. That led to every toffee manufacturer in Yorkshire—and there are a lot of them—sending humbugs to Harrogate. You could scarcely move in the dressing-room for the things. There were humbugs in tins, jars, cartons and packets—even a hundredweight sackful. The Yorkshire team each took some home for their kids, the secretaries and ground staff helped themselves but it still left a lot of tins and the sack untouched.

I was at a loss to know what the heck to do with them when someone suggested I offer them to a home for spastic children at Killinghall. So I rang the matron and she said she would be glad to have them—on condition that I came along to present them. Since the match had been washed out I went that afternoon. It was an experience that will live with me for the rest of my life. I nipped about, offering the humbugs to those poor children, when I came across a little lad who was encased in a thing resembling a clothes-horse made of tubular steel. If he wanted to move he had to grip one side and make it open to push one leg along, then grip the other to bring the second leg along. He walked to me. I said, 'How are you, son?' and he replied, 'I'm all right, Mr Trueman.' Then I asked him if he was doing well, and he said, 'Yes, I'll win the London to Brighton road race next year.'

That was too much for me. I filled right up. I couldn't stay any longer. The matron understood, told me she knew exactly how I felt and I left—swearing that if I did anything for charity then it would be for children. If that little lad is still alive I should like him to know that what he said to me on that wet afternoon more than twenty years ago has raised thousands of pounds for unfortunate and deprived children. Because when I got the chance to join the Variety Club, which exists solely to make money for children's charities, I jumped at it. I'm not going to say any more for two reasons—first, I haven't spent as much time working for the Variety Club as I would have liked because I have to work hard to live; second, I don't believe in advertising it like some of the big stars.

One set of stories about me which I should like to scotch started when I turned down invitations because they didn't include Enid. I do not ask for money to do charity appearances. Anything else, yes—and I'm not cheap. But I've never taken a penny for charity work yet, and I never will. I know some leading names who do, and they make me sick. Recently I had to become very angry with one Variety Club official who came on to me about a fortnight before the event. No one stands a chance of getting me at such short notice because I am heavily committed all the time. I work for the *Sunday People*, Yorkshire Television and the BBC on a regular basis, just for starters. But this man must have believed the stories and thought I was stalling for money. He made me an offer which I refused and I left him in no doubt what would happen if he insulted me that way again.

The divorce from Enid went through as quietly as possible for a man as well known as me. No dirty linen was washed in public, no third parties were involved. I went to ground in the Yorkshire Dales to avoid the press and everyone else. We were both reasonable about it. Today there are no grudges between us. We both know it was just one of those sad things that occur in life. Basically Enid is a very kind and generous person and I could never fault her as a mother to our children. I hope she will re-marry one day because she deserves a better life than she has had.

Eventually I found a house in an isolated spot on the fringe of the Dales and slowly started to rebuild my life, keeping in touch with the kids as often as possible. I still know every inch of the road to Scarborough backwards. I promised myself I would never again become tied to a woman, certainly never marry again.

You should never make promises like that to yourself. I'm glad I broke them.

Chapter 7

The Curse of the Truemans

None of the problems I faced in life, marital or otherwise, ever affected my performance on the field. The combined pressures of a marriage break-down and constant hostility from the cricketing establishment were enough to break any man's spirit, but when I walked to the end of my run-up there was only ever one thing on my mind—how to remove the opposition as quickly as possible.

In a phrase, I suppose I was determined to bloody well show them all. And the more the MCC put me down, the harder I tried. Some of those characters from the Long Room at Lord's never seemed to miss an opportunity to belittle me and tell me that I wasn't so quick or as good as the men of their day, which in some cases was shortly after underarm bowling went out of fashion. Gubby Allen, the England selector, once even humiliated me in public. He came down to the nets at Headingley the day before a Test against Australia, took out his handkerchief and put it down on the pitch at round about a length. Then he instructed me to try to pitch the ball on the handkerchief. An embarrassingly large crowd gathered to watch this exhibition of arrogance, and there was nothing I could do but grit my teeth and go through with it. He seemed to think he knew everything about fast bowling, having played as an amateur before I was born, and told me how to bowl out the Australians. For once I kept quiet because I'd just finished a long spell out in the cold and didn't want to get dropped again from the England side so soon. But Bill Bowes, who was among the spectators, said it all for me in his newspaper column the next day. He was not amused, and pointed out that Gubby Allen had no right to subject me to that kind of treatment, particularly since he never had any talent worth comparing with mine.

But I wasn't always able to keep silent and respectful during these confrontations and I made a lot of powerful enemies. I did my best to stay out of their way, but when they cornered me I usually gave them an honest opinion, which has always been my nature. The consequences were inevitable. Many times I met up with touring sides in Britain to be told how astonished they were about the number of times I was dropped. They wanted to know why, so I told them—for speaking my mind. I used to be 'sentenced' to one, two and sometimes three Test matches, depending on how seriously the selectors felt they had been insulted. In the fifties and sixties England had cricketers good enough to win and keep the Ashes like the Australians did in the forties. The reason we didn't was largely because of these men who didn't have the experience to run our national team.

Gubby Allen had another go at me in the nets later on in my career when I had taken over 200 Test wickets. This time I was practising at Lord's when he came up to me and asked why I took such a long run-up. He said that when he was bowling for England he only took half my run-up but was equally as quick as me. So I told him I'd studied Test match records and curiously he didn't seem to figure much. And my name was among the four fastest bowlers of the century—where was his? At that he seemed to become upset and said: 'We can't tell you youngsters anything.' I replied: 'That's not true, but *you* certainly can't tell me anything about fast bowling.'

Through the years there were dozens of minor clashes at cocktail parties and receptions when there was no way of avoiding these people. Some of them thought it clever to try to goad me, others tried to make a habit of addressing me as 'Trueman'. That's one thing I never could stand —it had to be 'Fred' or 'Mr Trueman', even if they were titled. Some of the honours distributed among the cricket establishment and a few favoured players were ludicrously ill-deserved and there was no way I was going to address some men as 'Sir', or their wives as 'Lady'. I had seen at first hand the way they had behaved on tour and elsewhere and they deserved no respect from me or anyone else. Neither did some of their wives, who were no ladies. Of course, they all knew how I felt—and why —which made matters worse. One man went so far as to tell me to be careful how I addressed him in future because he had just been given a title in the Honours List. Frankly I told him to get stuffed because as far as I was concerned he had got it off my back.

Generally the newer the title or honour, the more conscious they were of it. Some of the real aristocracy were far easier to get along with. His Grace, the Duke of Norfolk, for example. His appointment as manager of the Australian tour in 1962–3 astounded practically everybody in cricket and out of it. It was an amazing joke, but not really his fault—he was a very pleasant man, a real gentleman, and he was tremendously keen about cricket. But his qualifications for the job, which was so important, just did not exist. Perhaps the selectors thought they might harvest a couple of knighthoods, since he was so close to the Queen, often going racing with her and organizing many of the big ceremonial events. I was sure in my own mind that he accepted only because it would give him an ideal opportunity to arrange the Queen's subsequent tour of Australia, and watch his second favourite sport at one and the same time.

I just had one confrontation with the Duke. It happened at Melbourne when he called out, 'Trueman—come here!' I wasn't going to take that sort of treatment, not even from him. I told him I had a dog at home I spoke to like that, and I didn't care if he was the premier earl of England—he must address me properly. He took it very well indeed, and we finished up the best of friends having a drink together. When I set a new world record of 250 Test wickets on the New Zealand part of the tour he was the first on the field to congratulate me and shake my hand.

I had the sort of season for Yorkshire in 1962 which forced the MCC to pick me for that tour—153 wickets at an average of 17.75 each. It had taken 1,141 overs to get them, and I climbed on board the boat looking forward to a rest before I took on the Australians. So I wasn't too pleased when Ted Dexter, the captain, informed us that Gordon Pirie, who had run in the Olympics for England, was among the other passengers and he had offered to take charge of our training. All I wanted to do was sit in a deck-chair under the sun for a couple of weeks and forget about cricket until we got to the nets in Perth, apart from the occasional exhibition match along the way. Pirie seemed to me to be one of those athletes England was noted for in those days—enormously good at coming in second or third. He came to me and said I should stop eating steaks and go on a

9 Right after delivery

10 My action from another angle, 1956

11 I bowled for twenty years without even pulling a muscle

12 Against Lancashire, 1959. Another boundary —I didn't believe in wasting energy running

13   The England team
v. Australia at Birming-
ham, 1961

14   Headingley, 1961,
against Australia. I lead
the team in after five
wickets in the first
innings and six in the
second

15 Trying to sweep a ball from Mick Allen in a match for Yorkshire v. MCC at Lord's, 1958

16 Appeals all round when I bowled E. McMorris lbw in a match between England and the West Indies at Headingley, 1963

diet of nuts and lettuce like him. He also said he knew a
man who always ate food like that and he was still
chasing reindeer round the Arctic at the age of ninety-
five. I told him I had no intention of chasing reindeer at
any age, only Australians, and I needed steaks to do that.
Then he tried to have us running up and down on the
wooden decks of the ship, which was the worst thing a
fast bowler could do, because it tightened the calf
muscles. He also said he could devise some exercises for
me which would strengthen my legs, which had just seen
me safely through a thousand overs! That did it for me.
When he started going on about what this kind of
training had done for him I asked him if he had run
against a man called Vladimir Kuts. He said that he had,
indeed, so I said: 'Yes, and if I remember rightly he was
doing his lap of honour before you had crossed the
finishing line, so if that's what your training does for you
then you can count me out.' If the man had been able to
point to an Olympic gold medal it would have been
different. As it was, I concluded my final session with
him by expressing the hope that he could swim because
if he kept on bothering me he had every chance of
going over the side.

Ted Dexter was still very taken by the man and tried
to insist on the team following Pirie's instructions, but I
went to see Alec Bedser, the assistant manager and a
man who knew something about pace bowling, to explain
the damage pounding around the deck could do to me.

After that the voyage turned out to be the best I ever
experienced. We had a superb time socially, which was
exactly what we all needed after a full summer's cricket.
I set about organizing a skiffle group to enter the fancy
dress competition, made a double bass out of a tea chest,

97

decked it out in MCC colours and the Marylebone Calypso Club was born. Ken Barrington scrounged a pair of marraccas, Peter May, Colin Cowdrey and Tom Graveney joined in and we sang calypsos we had learned on the West Indian tours. I led the group, telling a few jokes and stories and introducing the songs, and we won the first prize. The Duke of Norfolk thought we were priceless and the ship's captain was so delighted that he added another half a dozen bottles of champagne to the prize. We bought some brandy and next day invited lots of people we had become friendly with to a party in my cabin—if ever there was a party, it always seemed to be in my cabin. Tom Graveney turned out to be as good as any barman at making champagne cocktails, even down to the sugar frosting on the rims of the glasses.

We got off the boat at Bombay to fly to Ceylon for a couple of one-day matches before the boat picked us up again for the final leg to Australia—where, just like the last time, it all went wrong again both on and off the cricket field. At the very first press conference, most of the questions were concerned about whether the Duke's racing colours would be seen on the Australian race tracks, and was Scobie Breasley going to come out and ride for him. Cricket was scarcely mentioned. Then Ted Dexter's wife came out to do some modelling, so the main interest switched to her. On top of this we were constantly surrounded by clergymen eager to meet David Sheppard, who had left cricket to become a man of the cloth but had got leave of absence to make a come-back. It was quite unnerving to see so many of them around the dressing-rooms and hotels. Soon all the newspapers and television programmes were full of where the Duke's horses were running, where David Sheppard was preaching and what Mrs Dexter was wearing. I became extremely fed up with all this, reasoning that we had come to Australia to play cricket, so I was frank when a newspaperman asked me what I thought about the tour up to then. I told him I was a bit confused, not knowing whether we were supposed to be playing under Jockey Club rules, for Dexter Enterprises or engaged on a missionary hunt. The man printed it rather prominently, and there I was—in trouble with the management again.

More harsh words were said when I was barred from endorsing products or making appearances and after-dinner speeches for money. I objected strenuously because I had worked hard against a lot of odds to become famous enough for people to want to pay me for using my name. It had become a regular and legitimate part of my living and I felt they had no right to take it away like that. There was certainly no way of making any money out of cricket alone, even at international level. I expected to be able to bank around £250 from my cricket earnings after this particular tour. There was a suggestion that I should throw any money earned on the side into a common pool, because Ted Dexter had been paid a few quid writing articles for a newspaper and put it all into the kitty. I rejected this idea. None of the others were likely to be asked to advertise anything, except maybe dog collars and horse liniment. I reckon the ruling cost me between two and three thousand pounds, which was a hell of a lot of money in those days. You can imagine how I felt.

Then my pride took a blow in the first Test at Melbourne when I had an inspired spell in terrible heat and took five wickets in the second innings (and three in the first). Modesty apart, I felt I had won the match for England—but when the English newspapers arrived I found that David Sheppard had been given all the glory.

He got a duck in the first innings, which nearly became a pair when he was dropped at slip before he had scored in the second. He survived to make a century and the newspapers were full of headlines like 'Sheppard Wins Test for England', and similar rubbish. Although I am one of them now, I am forced to say that the cricket writers rarely gave me any credit at this stage of my career, and sometimes tried to write me out of the team. I became sick and tired of reading how unlucky Brian Statham was not to get more wickets. But when I beat the bat and missed the wickets I was accused of inaccuracy. They just didn't know enough about the game. I gave Brian a hundred wickets start in Test cricket because of my long spell in the wilderness, caught him at 250 and then left him trailing.

There was another irritating incident at Melbourne, following a Saturday night party at a private house. Bill Johnston, the Aussie left arm medium pace bowler, was among the guests and we had a long and interesting talk about cricket in general and pace bowling in particular. We got on extremely well, in fact. But a few days later he came to me in a most agitated state to tell me there were stories circulating all over the place which claimed we had come to blows at the party. He wanted to know how the hell they could have started, since we hadn't even raised our voices. So I explained that ridiculous stories about me were ten a penny in Britain and it just meant the curse of the Truemans had hopped across to the Antipodes.

The Melbourne match was the first and last Test we won in Australia that winter. From then on a lot of tactical mistakes were made—vital ones—and I reckon that Ted Dexter must take the blame. I liked the man a lot and he could bat beautifully, but he was no captain of England. He had more theory than Darwin, but little practical experience to back it up. In fact, it was impossible for men like Dexter and Cowdrey to come straight from university into bad sides, like Sussex and Kent were in those days, and expect to learn much about captaincy. A side is poor because of the lack of ability in it, so if there's no one to bring on a potential captain, to teach him for several years by example and experience, how on earth can he suddenly acquire the knowledge and sheer craft needed to captain England? The Australians never made that mistake.

On the run-up to the Sydney Test, I was flown up from Tasmania ahead of the rest of the team to take a good look at the wicket and give an opinion. Now Sydney usually favours fast bowlers, but on this occasion there wasn't a blade of grass on the wicket. So I reported back that we should play an extra spin bowler—maybe even two—because it was going to be ideal for them and useless for pace. We had Ray Illingworth, Freddie Titmus and David Allen available, so we were strong in the spin department. Freddie Titmus had no doubts, either, when he saw the wicket. He turned to Ray and David in the dressing-room and said, 'Get your fingers loose, lads, because one of you two will be playing for certain.' But after Ted had deliberated he said that Len Coldwell, Brian Statham and myself had bowled so well at Melbourne that none of us could be dropped. I told him that the Melbourne Test had nothing to do with this one, that we were here to try to win the bloody series and he must drop a paceman—me, if necessary—because he could always put himself on as third seamer. The selectors refused. I was reduced to bowling off cutters at one end—but I couldn't pitch them slow enough to have much effect—whilst Freddie Titmus had a field day at the other end. If only he had been given the right support we would have won that Test easily. As it was, we lost.

The situation was exactly reversed when we came to Adelaide. There, it was obvious we needed a full three-man pace attack, but the selectors dropped Len Coldwell and brought in another spinner. Even with that handicap we might still have won if a couple of catches had been held off my bowling—including a chance from Richie Benaud, who was for ever being dropped off me before he had scored. David Sheppard, more at home in a pulpit than on a cricket pitch, didn't do much with the bat after Melbourne. I still proved the point about the state of the pitch by taking 4 for 60 in one innings and remained convinced that we would have taken the Ashes back to England if the right team had been picked. But the match ended in a draw, the series was stalemated into one each and three drawn and the Aussies hung on to the Ashes. It was heart-breaking.

On two occasions during that trip I thought I was reliving nightmares from the 1958-9 tour. Again, I had a dose of back trouble when we reached Brisbane and some specialist diagnosed a spinal deformity. He even declared I should go home at once and would probably never play cricket again. And then, just after bowling my heart out in a Test match, I was picked to go to Newcastle as twelfth man. This time it was worse. Trevor Howard, who was a good pal of mine, had invited me and some of the others to the Australian film première of *Mutiny on the Bounty*. I had never been to anything like that before, and it was a posh, black-tie affair. But I had to decline, and trail all the way to Newcastle. To make matters worse, Peter Parfitt broke a finger and I fielded under the blazing sun for three days—with another Test about to start.

I told them what I thought about that in simple and direct language. And I spoke my mind about the simple errors which had cost us the series. So did Ray Illingworth, another honest Yorkshireman, and when we arrived back in England we found that both of us had £50 docked out of the £150 good conduct bonus. It was the second time for me, and it was more than flesh and blood could stand. I had taken 34 Test wickets on that tour, broken a world record by becoming the first bowler ever to reach 250 and still they treated me like a naughty child. They never gave me any reason, on either occasion, and there was no way to appeal. I was so furious that I asked them to take the remaining hundred pounds and put it into the team pool, but they refused.

I was just as mad at Yorkshire because among all the messages and telegrams, including many from other English counties, when I got that 250th wicket in New Zealand there wasn't a word from Headingley. They eventually made the excuse that they were prevented from sending congratulations because Sir William Worsley, the president, was on holiday in Hong Kong at the time. I wondered what they did at Headingley when they wanted to go to the toilet and Sir William wasn't there to give permission.

Once again, the press made a big story out of the bonus stoppage. Shortly after it was announced, I was in a night club in Middlesbrough and said, as I had on another occasion, that it made me feel like refusing ever to play for England again. Who heard me I don't know, but the next day I was quoted in the newspapers—with one important difference. They made out I had refused to play for England ever again. Fortunately my old friend from the last West Indian tour, Walter Robins, was on the selection committee. He rang me after the stories were printed and said: 'What's all this, Fred?' I explained what had happened and told him that if I was picked for England next week, then I would be there. He said, 'Good—because you will be picked again.'

He kept his word. But sadly I was never selected again to go to Australia. It was a bitter disappointment, because I reckoned I was good enough for one more tour, even at my age. More than anything else, I wanted to beat the Aussies on their home ground. And if Brian Close had been the captain of the 1962–3 tour we would have brought back the Ashes for sure. He was a tremendous cricketer and the best county captain I ever played under. Although we had many rows over the years, we also had a basic affinity and the same object always in mind—to win for Yorkshire. He was unfairly blamed more than once for England's failures, most notably in the crucial Old Trafford Test against Australia in 1961. We were in a good position in the last innings and chasing victory. Peter May had given the order to force the pace and go all out to win the match. Both he and Dexter had gone, so the main responsibility fell on Brian. The wicket was good, he had just hit Richie Benaud for six and looked set. Norman O'Neill was sweeping up behind the covers, deep and square on the offside, to the right-handed batsmen. But he was fielding at fine leg to Brian, a left-hander, to stop him tickling it round the corner for four. Brian was in with a right-hander who pushed a single to the off, which O'Neill fielded. But when Brian took the next ball O'Neill hadn't gone back to his proper position and when he picked Benaud up on the leg stump and hit him round the corner it went straight to O'Neill, who took the catch forty yards out of position. It was a pure fluke, and a damned unlucky one at that. If O'Neill had been where he was supposed to be, the ball would have gone to the boundary and been hailed as a great shot. Instead the match was lost and Brian took a real hammering from the press, who accused him of throwing away his wicket and the Ashes along with it. Again, it showed how suspect their understanding of the game was. What they should have done was condemn Peter May who, when Benaud was bowling leg spinners round the wicket, played down the offside and was bowled round his backside. The ball hit his leg stump and Peter was so amazed that he just stood there, rooted to the spot. In fact, Wally Grout had to snap him out of it by saying: 'You're out, skipper, 'cause he's bowled you!' Playing down the wrong line was a bad mistake, and Peter May knew it. But no one said a word about it. Brian Close was dropped for the next Test, and so was I. They held me responsible for causing the rough patches which Benaud used to get some life out of the plumb wicket. I hadn't even bowled from that end—it was Ted Dexter and Jack Flavell. But any excuse would do. What made it harder to take was that the Headingley Test two weeks before was the only one we won in the series and I had taken eleven wickets.

Brian Close eventually got his chance to captain England five years later against the West Indian tourists. By that time he had settled in as skipper of Yorkshire, proved his worth by reorganizing the team and leading us back to the championship. There was no one better at reading a game, analysing the opposition and attacking them every inch of the way. I don't suppose the England selectors had much choice, but I'm sure they pretty quickly regretted appointing him, because Brian had his own ideas about who should play under him and didn't

keep them to himself. As it turned out, he didn't stay for
long.

Like me, Brian is a very even-tempered bloke, but
there are limits to anyone's patience. The day after
he had captained England in the second Test against
Pakistan at Nottingham, Yorkshire played Warwickshire
at Birmingham. The crowd got upset that day because we
tied up their batting and slowed the game down. The
ability to dictate play is the hallmark of a great side,
which Yorkshire had in those days. At lunch we were
filing through the members' enclosure—I was immediately behind Brian—when a man called him a bald-
headed bastard. Now no cricketer objects to people
shouting insults about his playing ability, but that was a
bit personal. Brian boiled over about the insult when he
got to the dressing-room and went back outside to find
the man and tell him what he thought of him—which
was only natural. But it seems he grabbed the wrong man
—well, that's what was claimed. He didn't hit him,
because Brian's not that daft. But the crowd turned
nasty from then on, and during the next day's play there
was still a bad atmosphere as we successfully forced a
draw and the Warwickshire supporters were deprived of
the unusual honour of beating Yorkshire, which had been
very much on the cards. As we came off the field at close
of play, a young man, who looked like a student, suddenly went for me with his umbrella. I got hold of him,
told him not to be silly or he would get hurt and I turned
to go into the pavilion. A second later two of the Yorkshire team shouted, 'Look out, Fred!' and I wheeled
round just as the umbrella was flailing down on me. I
ducked, grabbed it and smashed the thing. Then I got
him by the scruff of the neck, dragged him outside and
said: 'Now, let's see how brave you are without ten

thousand people round you.' I waited, but all he did was shake and whimper. So I just turned him round, kicked his backside and told him in somewhat basic terms to get out of my sight. I've known plenty like him—heroes in a crowd, but cowards when you get them on their own.

To my mind—and to that of any reasonable person who saw the incident—Brian Close did nothing that afternoon to bring either himself or the game into disrepute. But it was the chance the selectors seemed to have been waiting for. They stripped him of the England captaincy and gave it back to Colin Cowdrey for another winter in the sun against the West Indies.

Chapter 8

Batsmen and Bouncers

I don't know what it is about fast bowling, but it certainly brings out the worst in people. Spin bowlers can trundle up and down for twenty-five years and nobody pays anything more than polite interest, even at international level. Medium-fast bowlers, middle-order batsmen, all-rounders and wicket keepers come and go without causing so much as a ripple. Opening batsmen can stir things up now and again, largely because they are the principal enemies of fast bowlers and people get excited when they prosper against us. But the man who propels the ball twenty-two yards with all the power and pace he can muster is the one who drives people to extremes of reaction and judgment—spectators, press, selectors and administrators alike. They either want to give you the earth—like the amazing deal Jeff Thomson has signed with a Queensland radio station (and good luck to him)—or they are signing a petition to have you gelded in public.

In between, they indulge in cricket's great side-show, arguing about who is the fastest, who has the best action and who was like whom from the past—Harold Larwood, as ever, was generally the point of reference in all categories during my career. But the thing that fascinates them most of all is speed. Just who was the fastest bowler of all time makes for a futile argument, but it can raise blood pressures in every four-ale bar from Pudsey to

Perth. Godfrey Evans has been quoted as saying that he thought Frank Tyson was faster than me, but how can he be so sure? I am only certain of one thing: that I bowled faster over a longer period than anyone else on earth. Round about 1960 they even assembled scientific apparatus to measure the speed of the world's fastest bowlers. By that time I was nearly thirty and two or three years past my peak as far as sheer pace was concerned, and several friends of mine advised me not to put my reputation at risk against men like Wes Hall, who was around seven years younger than me. Only Brian Statham, by a few months, was my senior. The speed trials were carried out in England, Australia and the West Indies. Wes Hall registered 93 miles an hour through the air and 92 off the wicket. I did 92 miles an hour through the air and 93 off the wicket. Brian Statham and Peter Loader came into the eighties, but Alan Davidson of Australia only managed to get into the seventies. I can't remember all those who took part, but only Wes and myself topped ninety. Frank Tyson didn't enter because he had finished in top-class cricket by that time. If they had done the same trials when I was twenty-five I might have broken a hundred.

Frank Tyson was very quick—there can be no doubt about that—and he frightened the Aussies clean out of the Ashes in 1954-5, the tour I missed because of the nonsense in the West Indies. But I do not rate him as a great fast bowler. People infuriate me when they use the word 'great' so liberally, because to reach that level in my humble opinion you need to stay at the top for ten years. Frank, good though he was, had been and gone in two or three. I'm human enough to admit that I bitterly resented being dropped from the England team for him and, when Yorkshire played his county, Northamptonshire, I used to will myself to bowl faster and better than him to show the crowd, and the press, just who was boss. It made for some very keen matches because Frank always responded to the challenge. The dressing rooms were full of nervous batsmen.

When it came to playing for England I also very badly wanted to bowl better and take more wickets than the other pace bowlers in the team, and I considered myself in competition with Brian Statham during our long partnership. Curiously enough, very rarely did we both do well in the same innings. One of us would often get five or six wickets, the other just the odd one. But we both held the same views about batsmen—get them out as soon as possible so that we could put our feet up in the pavilion, have a smoke and watch our lads get on with it. Otherwise we were very different people. Brian—or George, as everyone called him—was very agreeable to everyone, so much so that the establishment could take advantage of him without much fear of retaliation. He never got dropped for speaking his mind. But there's no question of his stature as a fast bowler. He certainly proved his greatness, and I never begrudged him his success as many have suggested. Off the field there was no edge between us. We roomed together on tour, sat together on planes and spent a lot of time together socially.

If Brian had a fault, I think it was his lack of aggression. He never won a championship for Lancashire and only once took more than 150 wickets in a county season, whereas I bowled Yorkshire to the championship half a dozen times and topped the 150 wicket mark on four occasions. Had Brian been more like me—an arrogant bastard on the field—then I'm sure Lancashire would have done better.

Many people have accused me of being too aggressive,

of using the bouncer far too often. I disagree. I was forced to bowl short more often than I would have wanted to in order to get some life out of the slow, dead wickets which did so much to drive the crowds away in the sixties. If I could get one to lift round their heads now and again it served two purposes—to liven things up a bit for bored spectators and, more important, to sow a seed of doubt about the state of the pitch in the mind of the batsmen and perhaps push him into a mistake. Over the years I've hit a lot of people with the ball, sometimes catching them on the head and making them drop in their tracks. More than once I thought I had actually killed a man, and that always turned me sick to the stomach. But I never let it show, or the Trueman image would have collapsed for ever. If you are labelled a bastard you have to keep it up.

Only three times in my entire career did I deliberately set out in cold blood to injure a batsman. I did it because they had goaded me beyond endurance by the things they said to me both on and off the pitch. At the time I was only just starting my international career and was very confused by all the hostility.

In my prime I could have hit anybody I wanted. Those I did, apart from the three exceptions, happened either accidentally or in the heat of the moment—such as that occasion when that West Indian batsman persisted in calling me a white English bastard. And whenever I did injure someone, I knew there would be a reckoning—and I don't mean in the dressing room or pavilion, which I could cope with. It happened when I had to face the only man I suppose I was ever afraid of. My father. He would be waiting for me when I got back home with the words, 'You've been at it again, have you!' He certainly gave me some stick about clobbering people, did Dad. I would try and protest that it had been an accident, but he would point out that I risked damaging my career permanently. He was also worried that I might seriously injure a fellow professional with a wife and family to support.

One thing I never did was bowl bouncers at tail-enders. And it was nothing to do with the 'fast bowlers union'. I considered it beneath any fast bowler of Test status to use aggressive tactics with men who clearly had little or no skill with the bat, whether they were pace or spin bowlers. Many times I was asked to let a tail-ender have one round the ears because he was pushing steadily down the line and trying to bat out time, but I always refused, whatever the circumstances.

Apart from over-use of the short ball, I was often accused of erratic form—being brilliant one day and ineffective the next. Some thought it revealed a flaw in my bowling ability. Actually, it showed up a flaw in the knowledge and experience of the critics, who habitually flailed me whenever I returned figures like one wicket for ninety runs. Anyone who really knows cricket will tell you that a man can bowl superbly all day, get edged all around the ground and take not a single wicket. Then the next day on the same wicket he will get 6 for 20. But it helps to make cricket such a fascinating game, of course.

Quite often a rank bad ball will earn a wicket. The batsman can be so surprised at suddenly receiving a long hop that he fluffs it. It is also essential for a bowler to get the necessary support from the fielders. If they are dropping all the catches he can't succeed. It's often been said that I regularly savaged any fielder who put down catches off my bowling, but it's just another Trueman myth. Of course, I didn't enthuse but I had the sense to realize that the man responsible would be more upset than me. He was the one made to look foolish in front of a big crowd. There are stories which have me cursing and shouting, 'I'm playing this side on my bloody own', but my stock reply to any fielder apologizing for dropping a catch was, 'Don't worry, son—you didn't drop it very far. About eighteen inches, I'd say.'

Occasionally I was moved to a little sarcasm if a man kept on missing chances off my bowling, like the Reverend David Sheppard in Australia. I did tell him once to pretend it was Sunday and keep his hands together. And there was another, more celebrated occasion when a well-known England player not only dropped a vital catch off a batsman I'd been trying unsuccessfully to remove all day but let the ball go through his open legs for a four. When he apologized, adding that it wouldn't have been as bad if only he had kept his legs together, I made a crack which can only be repeated at stag nights. It also helped as much as anything to £50 being subtracted from my good conduct bonus.

To be fair, I must say that many outstanding catches were held off my bowling to redress the balance. A lot of the wickets I took for Yorkshire stemmed from the high quality of fielding which was expected at Headingley. Apart from exceptions like Tony Lock and Godfrey Evans, there just wasn't the same standard from the England team.

In fact I used to say that with Phil Sharpe at first slip, Brian Close at short leg and nine retrievers you could take the world on.

Chapter 9

In Pursuit of the Impossible

When I came back from the Australian tour of 1962–3 I was filled with the sort of burning ambition that I hadn't felt since I was a lad. All down the years I had played second fiddle to somebody. Brian Close was the first to get his Yorkshire cap, first to play for England. Brian Statham was the first to beat Alec Bedser's world record of 236 Test wickets and even Frank Tyson had been judged faster than me. But that season I had the chance not just to beat the lot of them. I had my sights on something which everyone said was impossible—300 Test wickets. Age wasn't on my side since I was in my thirty-second year, past retirement age for most fast bowlers, but I considered myself fit enough for at least another three years at international level, selectors willing.

At the start of the Australian tour I was chasing Alec Bedser's record along with Brian and he won the race with several to spare. And I was the one who took the catch off his bowling at Adelaide to put him up to 237 and his name in the record books. I passed the Bedser total myself later on during that tour but no one gets excited about the runner-up. Anyway, Brian had forged on to 242. But when the tour moved on to New Zealand and Brian left the party to go home I realized I had the chance to move ahead. At first I thought I was fated to

114

fail. I was injured whilst batting when the ball somehow got right round the pad and hit me in the back of the leg, so I missed the first Test at Auckland. On top of that there was more trouble within the team when the amateurs and professionals divided into two camps and I had a row with Colin Cowdrey. I felt I had some responsibility for the professionals since I was their senior man. The split was plain for all to see at one match in New Zealand when we had the use of two dressing rooms. The amateurs—Ted Dexter, Colin Cowdrey, David Sheppard and Alan Smith—used one and we professionals changed in the other.

It was a great pity about that first Test because the wicket turned out to be green. I'm sure I would have got among the wickets. I recovered in time for the second at Wellington, took another five wickets to draw level with Brian and went on to slip myself at Christchurch, grabbed ten wickets in the match and became the first bowler in the world to take 250 wickets. I was very pleased, of course, and celebrated accordingly. But the Alec Bedser record had been the one everyone was aiming at, so the next big one was really the magic 300.

When the West Indian tourists came in the summer of 1963 I couldn't wait to get at them. By then I had perfected a new, shortened run-up of twelve paces, instead of nineteen, and it was beginning to work like a dream. I lost a little speed—but was still as fast as anybody—and gained more control and effectiveness. I could make the ball move away that little bit later, and when the conditions were in my favour the results were devastating. For Yorkshire I began to take more and more wickets and I ended up top of every average in the country that season.

That Test rubber turned out to be one of the most

fascinating of all time and included that match at Lord's when the result hung on the last over. The West Indies needed one wicket to win, England six runs. It ended in the most nail-biting draw in the history of the game.

The West Indians led their attack with Wesley Hall and Charlie Griffith. Now Wes was one of the best fast bowlers of all time, with a superb, flowing action, but Griffith was the most curious quick man I've ever seen. Most of the England team knew him from the 1959–60 tour when he was just a run-of-the-mill bowler, coming off a short run-up with an action like Cliff Gladwyn, only not half as good a player. When the tourists came to play Yorkshire at Middlesbrough, Doug Padgett and Jackie Hampshire asked me how quick he was. I told them he was just medium fast and I couldn't understand the reports of him starting to knock wickets down all over the place. Yorkshire won the toss, elected to bat and a bit later Ray Illingworth came to me and said: 'Fred, you had better come and see this. You are not going to believe your eyes!' I went out and saw Griffith coming off a new, thirty-five yard run-up and sending them down like bullets. Except that his wasn't really a run-up, more of a waddle. But he clobbered both Doug and Jackie with the ball and they came off swearing he was the fastest thing they had ever seen. To me, the answer was obvious—he had started chucking the ball. Yorkshire went on to win that match despite Griffith, but England didn't fare as well.

The first Test at Old Trafford was a disappointment. The wicket had nothing to offer pace bowlers and I only added two wickets to my total. Griffith only got one and poor Brian Statham got hit all over the place for nothing at all. The West Indians were lucky enough to get us on a turning wicket and their spinners won it. Now we should have won that remarkable match at Lord's, but to my mind the tourists resorted to dubious tactics. Our batsmen were confidently chasing a win and then Hall and Griffith began to bowl at the ridiculously slow rate of about thirteen overs an hour. The lads became over-anxious, had to take unnecessary chances and wickets fell. If Brian and I had tried that sort of time-wasting we would have been hammered by the press and probably dropped for the rest of the series. But when I complained I was told in no uncertain terms to keep my big mouth shut.

Now I'll tell you something which has never been revealed up to now. During that match, when England were due to bat, I was having a quiet soak in one of the individual bathrooms at Lord's. The place was otherwise deserted. Then I heard voices in the corridor outside. And I found myself listening to R. V. W. Robins, chairman of the England selectors at the time, apparently talking to the two umpires about the suspect action of Griffith and the complaints which had been coming in from the various counties. I heard him say that the umpires should under no circumstances call Griffith for throwing. When they objected he explained that there was a lot of worry about racial tension in London and he feared a riot might be sparked off if Griffith was no-balled at Lord's. When I came out of the bathroom Mr Robins was waiting for me. He had heard me moving about. He asked me if I had overheard the conversation so I had to admit that indeed I had. Then he solemnly asked me to give my word never to disclose it. I promised I would keep silent for a time but told him that I thought it should be made public eventually if only to point out the handicap England had been playing under. I must say I was amazed that the chairman of selectors could give such guidance to umpires.

As a matter of fact I was torn between loyalty to my newspaper, the *Sunday People*, and the England team. It was the best story I ever dropped on. But I also knew that if I broke it I would certainly never play for England again and I wanted those 300 wickets more than anything. Two years later when Mr Robins, who is regrettably dead now, came to have a talk with me he referred to the incident and called it the best-kept secret in cricket. I repeated my intention to let it out one day.

So there we were—Griffith apparently chucking the ball and no one able to stop him. There wasn't even a word of complaint in the press, not even when they slowed the game down, and it occurs to me that editors might have been warned off too, because the South African controversy was at its height. It certainly went against the Trueman grain. I wanted no part of this silly English tradition of being able to lose graciously. I'm a Yorkshireman and I like winning graciously, or any other way as long as it's fair and honest. It also irritated me when I was told it was part of England's responsibility to put up with the behaviour of the West Indian supporters. The traditional White Man's Burden. I collected another reprimand at the end of the final Test at the Oval which the West Indians won to take the rubber. I watched with Billy Griffiths, the MCC secretary, as the West Indian crowd swarmed on to the ground and round the pavilion shouting, singing and dancing. Billy told me he thought it was a wonderful sight at the end of a Test series to see all the West Indian supporters coming to acclaim their side. I replied: 'Yes, and you should have seen the wonderful sight in 1960 at Trinidad when we were winning the series and the bottles started flying. Nobody came round the pavilion to acclaim us that day, except the crew of the Royal Yacht *Britannia*.'

We would have won that series in 1963 for certain had it not been for Griffith. Generally speaking, our batsmen won their battle with Wes Hall but there was no defence against Griffith. He bowled me out in the Oval Test when I had scored twenty and felt settled. Hall was at the other end and even with the new ball I was seeing him clearly. But when Griffith launched that one at me he went so wide of the crease and bent back so far that I thought he hadn't delivered at all. The lads told me that it passed the outside edge of my bat as I played down the line but it still knocked my middle stump out. It was the only ball in my life that I never saw from start to finish. His action was more of an amble than a rhythmical run, yet he was getting lift out of pitches which Wes and myself could do nothing with. The West Indian authorities must have got the message later because he eventually corrected his action, like Tony Lock once had to do. But the damage had been done. He took thirty-two English wickets on that tour, almost twice as many as Wes Hall, who was a far superior bowler.

I'm sure in my own mind that Charlie Griffith may have been partly responsible for Ken Barrington's heart attack in 1969 during a double wicket competition privately sponsored in Australia. Ken was partnering Colin Milburn, I was teamed with Basil D'Oliveira, the Pollock brothers of South Africa played, Bill Lawry was with Doug Walters, Sobers was with Hall—and Griffith came with Rohan Kanhai. The idea of the double wicket game is for pairs to play each other, batting and then bowling a limited number of overs with all the others fielding until their turn comes. If one partner is put out he has to stay and run with the survivor until he goes or the overs run out. We played a series of five with an accumulative points system in Sydney, Victoria, Brisbane, Adelaide and Perth.

Now Ken had written a book in which he had accused Griffith of throwing and also declared he would never play with him again. He's a nervous person is Ken and he got more and more uptight and frustrated because we had to share dressing rooms and travel together. It all got very tense. When we arrived in Victoria he collapsed and couldn't play any more. I had to take over from him in the semi-final with Colin Milburn and we won that day, but Sobers and Hall won the final.

I suppose in a way I benefited personally from the unfair situation in 1963. I became so angry that I found new reserves of strength. In two successive Tests I took a total of twenty-three wickets and ended up with thirty-four to add to my collection. It was my most successful Test series. I tore the West Indian batting apart in the Edgbaston Test, taking six wickets in less than an hour and winning the match for England. My bag would have been higher but for a mysterious injury which prevented me bowling in the second innings of the final Test. For no apparent reason I got a crippling pain under the ball of the heel of one foot which not even a cortisone injection could shift. I had it X-rayed but there was no sign of a break or a tear, and what made the whole thing more curious was that several other fast bowlers suffered exactly the same ailment at that time, including Brian Statham and Richard Hutton. It lasted for about three weeks, then went as suddenly and inexplicably as it came.

The following year it was the turn of the Australians

to tour England and I couldn't have arranged it better myself. If I was to get 300 wickets I wanted the last one to be an Australian. I was just sixteen short. I prepared carefully, got myself as fit as possible and kept working on the short run-up which had done more than anything to make 1963 my best-ever season. In the first Test at Nottingham I nailed Ian Redpath very early with a good one, which moved off the seam as he tried to push me towards mid wicket and clipped the top of his off stump.

Fifteen to go and all the matches still to play. But when we came off for lunch a couple of the selectors told me that my short run-up was going to be no good against the Australians. I reminded them about the thirty-four wickets against the West Indians, all taken on the shorter run, and pointed out that they were an even better batting side than the Aussies. But they insisted and like a bloody fool I agreed to go back to the longer run which I hadn't used for eighteen months. I found that I'd practically forgotten how, lost my rhythm and couldn't pitch the ball properly. It was dropping short and Norman O'Neill gave me a real hiding, hooking me all over the ground. I still got two more wickets but for once I was glad when the rain washed out the match for a draw.

I was a worried man when the next Test began at Lord's because I knew my place was in jeopardy after that performance. I went back to my short run, took five wickets for less than fifty runs and would probably have put England one up had the weather not closed in again. Eight wickets to go and three more matches to play— I felt nothing could stop me. The next was in front of my own people at Headingley and I would have given a lot to achieve the 'impossible' in front of them. But it turned out to be a totally frustrating experience and, according to some experts, the worst Test match I ever played.

But they don't know what was going on at the wicket. I blame Ted Dexter, the skipper, for what happened. He gave the impression he knew more about fast bowling than me.

We were in a strong position with only Peter Burge to get out, apart from the tail-enders. I knew I could remove Peter with a bouncer but Ted seemed to think otherwise and refused to allow me to place a fielder where I wanted one. Maybe I shouldn't have persisted in dropping the ball short, but Burge was doing exactly as I expected—hitting them in the air over square leg. But there was no one there to take the catch and he started to amass runs. I got his partner, Neil Hawke, but Burge was still there the next day. By that time the situation had been reversed and Australia were placed in a winning position. And then a substitute fielder, Alan Rees of Glamorgan, came on and I got my way at last. I placed him where I had wanted a fielder from the start and sure enough Burge, who had scored a century, hit another bouncer straight down Alan's throat. He didn't even have to move to take the catch. I could have had Burge out the day before and the match would have been won. Instead, we lost and it turned out to be the key match of the series.

I was held responsible and got dropped for the next Test—three short of the 300. They picked Fred Rumsey and John Price for Old Trafford and the Aussies set about them with murderous ease. Bobby Simpson scored 316 at the head of a queue of happy Australian batsmen. As for me, I had a quiet laugh wondering what was going through the minds of the selectors. They couldn't blame me that time. But I was furious when a newspaper printed a picture of me, pint in hand, laughing my head off. I don't suppose the selectors bothered to check, but it had actually been taken three years earlier in Australia. Largely because they had no option, they recalled me to the Oval.

England batted first in that match and our batsmen failed once again. And when I tried to get amongst the Aussies nothing went right. Two or three catches were put down off me, I was taken off and I thought that I might not make it after all. Just before lunch on the Saturday I saw Ted Dexter standing at the wicket looking a bit vacant, ball in hand. I asked him what he was going to do, and he said he was thinking of putting Peter Parfitt on to bowl. I said, 'No, you're not,' took the ball off him and put myself on. There was time for one over before lunch and with the fifth delivery I knocked back the middle stump of Ian Redpath. With the sixth and last I had Graham McKenzie caught at slip.

Just two balls had brought me out of disgrace. Now they were all clapping and cheering as I went back to the pavilion, on a hat trick for my 300th Test wicket. The news was spread by radio and television (which broke into its scheduled programmes to stay with the match) and the Oval was packed when we came out again. When my turn came I remembered that occasion twelve years previously when I so desperately wanted to take a wicket with my very first ball in Test cricket. The same feeling swept over me, only multiplied ten times.

Neil Hawke, an old pal, faced up to me. Before he did so he said: 'Well, F.S., I wouldn't mind being the 300th I suppose.' I tried like hell to make the fairy story come true, but I hadn't bowled for forty minutes, which didn't help. The ball went just wide of his off stump. I'd aimed at off and middle. The suspense went on until we took the new ball when, in my first over, I whipped down an outswinger—my favourite delivery—and Neil edged it into the hands of Colin Cowdrey at slip. Neil was the first to congratulate me. To mark the event I gave him a bottle of champagne and it's still on his sideboard in Adelaide, untouched.

A lot of people have asked me what went through my mind at that moment and they are always surprised when I tell them: the next wicket. There was another one to get, and I wanted it. I took it in the next over. The full significance of the occasion didn't hit me until much later in the dressing room when I was being interviewed by press and television. They were still clamouring round when suddenly I knew I had to get away and be on my own. I excused myself, went to a bathroom, put the bolt on the door and let the tears come.

I had done it, despite all.

The Yorkshire Committee didn't seem to be too impressed by the feat. Once again there was no telegram from the club among the cartload which arrived that day, although one committee member did send one privately. Eventually Headingley did decide to make me a presentation to commemorate the 300th and bought a silver tea service—with a little help from my own wallet. Sir William Worsley presented it to me at the annual Yorkshire lunch and when he examined it afterwards spotted something which had puzzled me. It hadn't been inscribed, although the club had bought it four months previously. Sir William became annoyed. 'How the devil will anyone know in the future what it was bought for?' he said. So they hurriedly took it back and kept it for another nine weeks.

And I was somewhat taken aback when the county secretary, John Nash, told me I was very lucky to get it. Burglars had ransacked the offices during the winter and taken the safe and other valuables. But they had ignored my tea service which was in a box on top of a wardrobe!

The England selectors didn't change their attitude towards me either. They passed me over for the winter tour of South Africa, which was very galling. Apart from the fact that South Africa was the best trip of the lot for weather, scenery and social life (so I was told—I never had the chance to find out at first hand), I badly wanted to push on well into the fourth century. I was still the best fast bowler in England and South African wickets were easier to get than Australian. It was suggested later that the selectors wouldn't let me go because of the delicate political situation over there, that they were afraid I would speak out of turn and whip up a storm. If that's true, then it was damned unfair. I've been to South Africa more than once and got along splendidly with everybody, black and white. I was also told by a senior member of the South African cricket authority that he had pleaded with the England selectors to send me on that tour, saying, 'If Fred comes we shall fill the grounds.'

The MCC gave me a different reason at the time. They said they considered me too old at thirty-three. But it was soon proved to be a lie. I had been replaced by Tony Nicholson, my Yorkshire partner, but he injured his back and couldn't go. In his place they picked Ian Thompson, a reasonable medium fast bowler who got his hundred wickets for Sussex each year. And he was two or three years older than me!

It felt like 1953 all over again.

The New Zealanders and South Africans had a split tour of England the following year—three matches each, starting with New Zealand. I got back in the team and took another six wickets. That made it 307 and I thought there were plenty more to come. But that was it. I never played for England again.

I was dropped from the second half of the series because the South Africans pulled a real con trick with the selectors. Eddie Barlow, their opening bat, told me about it afterwards. At the cocktail party held to welcome them at Lord's they told the selectors that they thought both Brian Statham and I were over the hill, having played against us at county level. It was an old Aussie dodge, because I suspect they thought they had a better chance of beating England if we weren't playing. The New Zealanders reckoned that the MCC were vulnerable to this sort of propaganda—it was said Australia had helped pick the England team for years. The classic case was when Don Bradman went on about Doug Wright being the finest leg spin bowler he had ever played against. They kept picking Doug, and Bradman kept knocking double centuries off him.

Both Brian and myself were dropped.

Over the years I estimate I was robbed of around thirty-five Tests. I should have been the first man ever to play a hundred times for England. I could have set a record which would have stood for ever—450 Test wickets, at least.

I know that Lance Gibbs crawled past my record against the Australians in January 1976. Spinners do have an advantage over fast bowlers because they can go on until they qualify for the old age pension, if the selectors allow it. The other thing, of course, is that his wickets have cost him more runs than mine—I took my wickets, he bought his.

Chapter 10

I Could Have Been Skipper!

By the time the 1961 season started I felt it was time Yorkshire gave me a benefit. After all, I had been bowling for them since 1949 and, as I pointed out to the committee, twelve years was an unusually long time for a fast bowler to wait for a bonus.

But Brian Sellers told me I would have to wait a bit longer because Brian Close took precedence over me and he hadn't yet had a benefit. I couldn't argue with that, although Brian joined Yorkshire at the same time as me, but complained that I was being pushed back two seasons which didn't seem fair to a man who was bowling more overs than the spinners. I'd put the work in—why hadn't they, in getting things properly organized?

In those days Vic Wilson was captain of Yorkshire. He might have been good enough to be a county cricketer, but in my opinion he was scarcely an inspiring captain. He often bowled me so hard that I thought I would turn into a grease spot. But for years we had travelled to matches in the same car and I thought we were good enough mates. So you can imagine how I felt when, in the middle of my benefit season in 1962 when everyone was supposed to be pitching in to make it as successful as possible, he had me sent home to be disciplined from the Somerset match at Taunton. I will never forgive him for it.

The day before that match started, I had captained the Players in the very last Gentlemen v. Players match at Lord's. Driving back through the holiday traffic I missed a turning and found myself in Exeter, so it was after two o'clock when I finally arrived at the hotel, completely knackered. Because of some confusion over my room number I didn't get the morning call I'd booked and slept on. I woke up in a panic at 10.40 a.m. and broke another world record by arriving at the ground, shaved and ready, at 11 a.m. Players were supposed to report at 10.30 a.m., but Vic Wilson was aware that I'd got to bed very late through no fault of my own and there was still time to spare before he was supposed to announce his team. But he dropped me, ordered me to report to the Yorkshire Committee the next day and told the press that he had been forced to discipline me. The press made a real meal of the incident and publicity like that was exactly what I wanted to avoid in my benefit year. I was so livid I very nearly quit Yorkshire for another county.

As Yorkshire took on Somerset I had to trail 400 miles back to Headingley and appear before Brian Sellers and the rest of a special committee. To my surprise they accepted my explanation. They paid my expenses and even sanctioned my match fee.

I wasn't sorry to see Vic Wilson go at the end of the season. He retired, and handed over to Brian Close. I was criticized for refusing all appeals to contribute to Vic's farewell present, but I felt I was more than justified. I'm not a hypocrite. I took my benefit at Sheffield, the ground nearest Maltby, and when they counted up all the takings from the other functions organized on my behalf I had nearly ten thousand pounds to put in the bank. A good benefit is vital to a cricketer so he has something to lean on when the years catch up with him

17 Time to relax, Scarborough Festival

18 With my daughter Karen and Bill Bowes, former Yorkshire and England fast bowler, 1963

19 Ringmaster with Billy Smart's Circus in a charity effort for
the Variety Club of Great Britain in the 1960s

20 The twins' first taste of cricket (Rodney and Rebecca)

21 The twins' first birthday, 1966 (Rodney and Rebecca)

22 The Yorkshire team v. Surrey at the Oval, 1965

23 Full of intentions —going in to bat at Park Avenue, Bradford, 1966

and he has to give up the game and try to find a job with no qualifications other than the ability to bat or bowl. There is no way of building up capital from his retainers and match fees, however successful he may be.

The Taunton débâcle wasn't the last time Yorkshire tried to humiliate me. Worse was to follow. As late as 1966, when I was thirty-five years old and had served Yorkshire loyally for seventeen consecutive seasons, I received the worst insult of the lot. The occasion was a match against Lancashire at Sheffield. I had just come off after bowling solidly for an hour and taking six wickets and was going to field at mid-on when Tony Nicholson prepared to bowl. I was still trying to get my sweater on and called out to Tony, asking him to give me a chance and hang on a bit. But he carried on, bowled at the leg stump instead of the off and the batsman pushed the ball towards mid wicket. I was the only fielder covering from square to deep mid-on and it was obvious they would get one run very easily. So I didn't exert myself to reach the ball—just made sure they wouldn't get a second.

When I got back to the dressing room Brian Sellers was waiting for me, clearly an angry man. He accused me of not trying, which was ridiculous after I had bowled myself silly to get six wickets. And then he called me a bastard in front of everybody. Now I had learned to keep my temper, but sitting there in the dressing room was my elder brother Arthur, a big, proud man. The chairman was the luckiest man in the whole of Yorkshire that day because Arthur is a hard man and very strong from working in the pit and proud of his younger brother, and it would not have surprised me if he had struck him there and then. I managed to smooth things over. If he had said that a few years before I would probably have thumped him myself, but by then I was the senior professional and had to try to set an example.

Anyway, Brian Sellers decided to make it a big issue and called a committee meeting to consider disciplinary action. The day they met and decided to suspend me 'for not trying' I was captaining Yorkshire against Leicestershire. Ray Illingworth split his finger in the second innings, Don Wilson's finger also became too sore for him to bowl so I ended up bowling cutters—and took another six wickets to win the match! The crowd was really on my side as the news of the committee's decision broke, shouting out: 'That's the best possible answer you could give 'em, Fred!'

As the rest of the Yorkshire team set off to play the next match at the Oval I went home, suspended for a match without pay. But it was a very profitable suspension. I appeared on a couple of television programmes, was interviewed on radio several times, spent a few days with the family and made a tidy sum. If I had gone to the Oval match, spoiled incidentally by a dead wicket, I would have received a £22 match fee. Since we still had to pay all our own travelling, food and hotel expenses I would have been lucky to end up with £6. Like I said, there was no money to be had out of cricket when I played. On top of match fees, we only got a monthly retainer of £24, plus a £2 bonus for a win.

That Oval wicket was typical of the pitches being prepared in the early sixties. I don't know exactly what the groundsmen were doing to make them so lifeless— probably watering them and using a light roller—but they were hell to play on. Nobody benefited, neither batsmen nor bowlers of any kind. A lot of the skill in cricket is knowing how to deal with wickets of all kinds— how to get the most out of a sticky dog if you are a spinner or the best way to use a flier to advantage if you are a pace bowler. And batsmen had to learn how to cope with an awkward wicket, out-fox the bowler and get runs. But they all went dead during that period and made everybody look ordinary. I told one or two groundsmen to dig the bloody things up and bury them somewhere else.

I'm certain those pitches were basically responsible for driving away the crowds from county cricket. Nobody wants to pay to be bored out of their minds watching a match grind to a draw over three days. They want action, excitement and a result.

If anyone could win matches on those pitches it was Yorkshire, of course. Brian Close was a skipper who believed in leading from the front, and to try and force the pace he would place himself in suicidal positions a few feet from the bat. But it meant that you could hardly refuse to play there yourself if he had just shown you how. Brian had an outstanding cricket brain and never stopped thinking and talking about techniques and tactics. He wasn't the only one with this kind of knowledge and enthusiasm, and the Yorkshire Committee were moved to say that they had an unusual abundance of potential captains in the side at the time. They thought that both Ray Illingworth and myself were good enough for the job.

During the three seasons up to and including 1968, when we scored a hat trick of championships, I captained Yorkshire on many occasions when Brian was unfit to play. Ironically, Brian, who frequently took to the field with bandages on his knee or ankle from the early sixties onwards, decided in May 1968 to drop me from the team. This hadn't happened to me, apart from reasons of 'discipline', since I was a colt and the explana-

tion he gave was laughable really. He said I was unfit!
Now it's almost impossible to sprint up and down all day
for years and not be fit. I didn't need to be strapped up
like him. What's more, the day before he dropped me I
had bowled out Gary Sobers, second ball, for a duck.
That wasn't a bad performance for an 'unfit' man,
considering that Sobers was in his prime.

But what really hurt was the way the news was delivered. When I turned up for the match against Warwickshire at Middlesbrough it was Alan Smith, the
opposing captain, who came to tell me I was twelfth
man. Brian admitted later that he hadn't the heart to
tell me himself.

I suppose that incident persuaded me to start thinking
about retirement in 1968. By then I had been obliged
by advancing years to resign from fast to medium fast,
except for the short burst. Mind, I was still a hell of a
lot faster than some alleged quickies, then and now. I
was still bowling an enormous number of overs, far too
many for a man of my age and I began to have sleepless
nights because my legs ached so much. Once again I
was overdue for a benefit. Brian Close had his second,
but the committee informed me they had given 1968
to somebody else. It was truly disheartening.

To be fair to Brian, he did urge the committee to give
me a cheque for at least £1,000 as compensation, but
they refused. Blocking my second benefit is something I'll
always hold against Yorkshire, because I was popular
enough to smash all the benefit records. It would have
made me £15,000 richer.

Towards the end of the 1968 season I had one of the
greatest days of my life. I captained Yorkshire at Sheffield
against the Australians, who were playing Lawry,

Chappell, Redpath and their other stars for safety, and we beat them by an innings and sixty runs. It was only the second time Yorkshire had achieved such a momentous victory—the first was in 1902. After that match I sat back and considered the situation. I was coming up to thirty-eight, no longer Trueman the Terrible but still at the top with a side which had just thrashed the Aussies and was sure of the championship again. I had seen Yorkshire deal cruelly with older players, discarding them like so much rubbish regardless of the loyalty they had shown over the years. Johnny Wardle was a prime example. I had bowled 16,470 overs during twenty years of first-class cricket and taken 2,304 wickets. This meant that I had sprinted more than two million yards, or nearly thirteen hundred miles, in the service of Yorkshire and England (and walked the same distance back), which must be some kind of record. I had set a world record for Test wickets taken and had been Yorkshire's most successful fast bowler ever. And yet I knew there were men on the Yorkshire Committee who would have enjoyed sacking Freddie Trueman. So I decided not to give them the option.

I said nothing for a long time after I came to my decision, because soon afterwards Brian Statham announced that he would retire at the end of the season. I thought I would watch carefully and see what happened to him. And when Brian walked out for his last match at Old Trafford it was an overwhelmingly emotional moment. I knew immediately that I wouldn't be able to stand the same thing. It would have reduced me to tears, and I wasn't going to allow that to happen in public. I made up my mind to go quietly, which confounded a lot of my enemies who predicted that I would go round every ground playing to the crowd for applause. I announced my retirement well after the end of the season and there was no big farewell.

I dealt with the matter very carefully. To begin with, I wrote a very polite letter—I didn't want to leave the club under a cloud. Then I rang Sir William Worsley, father-in-law of the Duke of Kent by then, and asked for an appointment because I thought the president of Yorkshire should be the first to know.

Now Sir William was one man in cricket administration I respected completely. In fact, I thought him the only real gentleman in the game, apart from the Duke of Norfolk. He took a personal interest in my career from the start, encouraging me to score more runs by offering to give me £10 for my first century and paying up when it happened. When I got my thousandth first-class wicket against Hampshire at Leeds he was waiting at the top of the pavilion steps to congratulate me. The same thing happened when I clocked up two thousand. A couple of handshakes and a cheque for £10 may not sound much, but they meant a lot to me.

When I rang him that Saturday evening he said straight away: 'It must be important—come round now.' When I arrived I came straight to the point and told him I was getting out of the game. He said: 'Oh no —don't do that. You can go on for years yet and you are probably one of the greatest medium fast bowlers in the world.' I told him I was sorry but my mind was made up and handed him the letter. He read it, said he was most moved by it, but couldn't accept it. I didn't understand at first. And then he delivered a real bombshell.

He said: 'We are to hold a meeting next week and you will probably be offered the captaincy of Yorkshire!'

You have to be a Yorkshireman to understand what the position of county captain really means. It's the supreme accolade, much more coveted than the captaincy of England and much harder to get. When I recovered my powers of speech I told Sir William that if someone had only hinted about the possibility I would have been delighted to play on for another two or three years. But it was too late—I had announced my retirement in the *Sunday People*. He asked me to ring in and stop the story, but it was too late. The early editions were already coming off the presses. So by a couple of hours I missed being captain of Yorkshire. I'll regret it for the rest of my life.

Later the same night I drove to the home of Brian Sellers, gave the letter of resignation to him and had a couple of drinks. He said that perhaps I had helped the Yorkshire Committee out of a difficult situation. He didn't elaborate, but I did wonder whether they were going to sack Brian Close from the captaincy and give him the choice of either playing under me or leaving. Now there can be no doubt that Brian was a brilliant captain—the records prove it—but if he left himself open to criticism, it was over his attitude to youngsters. He was loath to bring them on and give them a chance. I tried many times to persuade him to change his policy, but he said they would have to fight their way into the team, like we had to.

Unfortunately the Yorkshire side was becoming rather elderly. Brian and I were both pushing thirty-eight, Ray Illingworth was thirty-six, Doug Padgett was into his thirties and it was clear that an injection of youth was badly needed. In the years to follow, the failure to blood youngsters into the senior team led directly to a dismal run of failures. If I had taken over as captain I think I might have prevented that. To begin with, I would have done everything in my power to persuade Ray Illing-worth to stay. He would have made a vast difference. All Ray wanted was a contract for two or three years to protect himself and his family until he organized a new career to enter when he became too old to play. It wasn't much to ask, but Yorkshire in their wisdom refused him and he left to play for Leicestershire where he went from strength to strength, becoming captain of both his county and his country and winning back the Ashes in Australia. Ray was one of the finest all-rounders in the world for years but, significantly, he didn't become a regular member of the England side until he was over thirty-five and no longer playing for Yorkshire.

Not long after he had gone it became clear that Yorkshire needed him desperately and I think he would have made a magnificent captain of his native county. I'm sure I would have been happy to hand over to Ray after two or three years in the job myself. As it was, even Brian Close had gone within two years of my retirement. And the way he was removed was a disgrace, even by Yorkshire standards. Here was a man who had played for Yorkshire since he was a kid, put in twenty-three years of dedicated work, brought honours and championships to the club, only to be phoned up, told to report to Headingley immediately and given half an hour to make up his mind whether to resign or be given the boot. Not just deprived of his captaincy, but thrown out of the club altogether. It broke his heart.

Naturally he was snapped up by another county and proved he had years of top-class cricket left in him. He was made skipper, of course, and went on to get another benefit—three in twenty-seven years compared to my one in twenty years!

It was a tragic time for Yorkshire cricket. No team can stand to lose so many international players all at the same time, particularly when there's no competition from the second team. It led to enormous trouble among supporters and ordinary members who refused this time to take it quietly. An influential group got together, formed an action committee and gave the Yorkshire hierarchy a real thrashing. Jack Mewies, my friend and solicitor, was a leading member but I stayed out of it. I was a newspaper columnist and had to take a neutral position, although I supported them privately. As a journalist I went to one meeting attended by Brian Sellers and he astonished me by declaring in his speech how pleased he was to see me there. He went on to say that the committee didn't realize when I was playing just how good a captain I was and how much I had done for the youngsters in the club. At this a rather hostile crowd began to shout 'Why didn't you make him captain, then?' but he didn't reply. I don't suppose he was in any position to reveal that his committee had intended to do just that.

Oddly enough, I got along with Brian Sellers much better after I left the club. But when I was playing I found him to be a man who would never listen to the other side's argument. Captaining Yorkshire would have been no joy ride—I had evidence of that on the occasions I took over from Brian Close. The committee sometimes tried to make decisions about players at a distance of 300 miles and try to force them on the captain. But I wouldn't let them. I had positive ideas about how to lead a team and they weren't going to work with the continual threat of interference by telephone or post from Leeds. I learned that from Ronnie Burnet.

I remember the first time I took over from Brian when

we went to play Somerset at Bath—and lost. In Yorkshire eyes this was a disaster because Somerset was hardly a good team. I let the players know what I thought about their performance in basic terms when we arrived in Swansea the following day. From then on I had no trouble. They accepted my leadership. In return I put their interests and welfare first. If we needed to go for runs then I would grab the bat and set an example. If there was a bad room in the hotel then I took it. I didn't try to interfere with their private lives, telling them I couldn't care less what they did between the hours of 6.30 p.m. and 11 a.m., but I would be very concerned if they weren't fit and on form between 11 a.m. and 6.30 p.m. When we got all the guide lines sorted out they gave me all the loyalty I needed and I supported them in return.

On one occasion I received a letter on green paper from Headingley telling me to drop two players and send them home. Two replacements were on their way. I refused to go along with it and kept the team together. For that I received another reprimand and was told that a green letter meant that the instruction carried the full authority of the committee and had to be obeyed. I asked them how the hell they could know what was going on in the field from their easy chairs in Leeds.

There was another confrontation at Leeds just before we tossed up at the start of Jimmy Binks's benefit match against Surrey. They wanted me to drop Doug Padgett for Barrie Leadbetter. Now I knew Doug was the best player in the side and I refused to do it. Brian Sellers was furious and the match was held up for ten minutes whilst he telephoned another official to see if I had the right as captain to override him. Apparently I had, and Sellers turned to me and said: 'You've won this battle, but you won't win the next!' What he meant by that I didn't know. But I will say this for him—after Doug Padgett had scored sixty-odd and we had beaten Surrey by an innings, he came to me and said, 'Well done. I'll be in the bar with a pint for you.' I went, and we had a chat, but I could tell the affair still rankled. He had been defeated and he wasn't used to it, but he bore no malice.

If only men like him would use their power with more discretion, advising instead of trying to dictate. They should try to encourage, not frighten players. I'll never forget the occasion in 1966 when I captained Yorkshire against Middlesex at Lord's. I had gone down to see Freddie Titmus, the Middlesex skipper, to exchange team sheets. He asked me to hang on for a couple of minutes because two of his lads were having fitness tests. So I began to chat to John Murray and Peter Parfitt when suddenly three England cricketers jumped to attention as though they were still in the forces, thumbs down their seams. I wondered what the hell was going on until they began to signal with their eyes to one side. I turned round—and saw Gubby Allen walking down the corridor towards us. I could scarcely believe my eyes. Three world class players rigid at attention because Gubby Allen was entering the room. So I said: 'You carry on. I'll come back and see you later when you're off parade', and left.

I had one more confrontation with Gubby Allen later on when my book of instruction for young cricketers was published. He told me that he couldn't agree with everything I had written about the techniques of bowling. I used my stock answer and told him to look in the record book. My name was still at the top of the list.

When I came off the Yorkshire payroll in November 1968 the committee decided I must have a farewell present. Since they owed me a benefit I hoped they might be generous this time. I was, after all, Yorkshire's third most successful bowler of all time—third only because George Hirst played until he was forty-five and Wilfred Rhodes hung on until the age of fifty-two! But I ended up having to add £120 of my own money to make their token of appreciation for twenty years' hard labour amount to something. They had set a limit of £100. I chose a Georgian silver cruet set which bears no inscription.

When they handed it over, that was it. The next day you would have thought that a fast bowler called Freddie Trueman had never played for Yorkshire. There was no welcome at Headingley for me any more. The year after I retired I dropped in to ask for a couple of tickets for a Test match and a secretary asked me what made me think I was entitled to tickets. I told her that 67 Tests and 307 Test wickets seemed a fair reason, but I would be happier if she stuck them up her backside and walked out.

Now if I turn up at Old Trafford, Edgbaston or the Oval they go out of their way to make me welcome. Yet in the seven years since I retired I haven't been in the offices at Headingley more than three times. I don't get invitations to the official functions and dinners and when they asked the press to the annual luncheon in 1975 I wasn't included, despite my official credentials as a sports journalist. Up until January 1976 I was not even a member because I wouldn't pay the subscription in view of the treatment they have handed me. I know they have now made me an honorary life member, but I am still bitter.

However, I remain a loyal Yorkshireman and follow the progress of the team closely. I'm sad when they are making a mess of things and elated when they win. I can't say I'm too enthusiastic about Geoff Boycott as a captain, magnificent though he may be with the bat. I'm not sure he has the ability to handle players and win their loyalty, and he seems to have some strange ideas. He knows what I think because I've told him personally. On the other hand, I feel that basically he's a good lad and genuinely wants to take Yorkshire back to the top again. And I do concede that he has had nothing much to play with. You can't win championships with the squad he has to lead. I don't expect Yorkshire to be the cock county again until around 1979.

But I do take heart from the appointment of some new committee men who seem to have a proper understanding of the game, a modern outlook and the interests of the club at heart. I reckon that when I was playing, most of the committee members in the game would have become bankrupt in six weeks if they had tried to run their businesses like they ran their county clubs.

I don't plan to try and win election myself to the inner sanctum at Headingley. Several of the old brigade remain and I don't fancy spending half my life trading abuse across a polished oak table.

Chapter 11

Life Without Cricket

I faced up to retirement with much more confidence than others before me. I had written for the *Sunday People* since 1957 and they were keen to go on employing me. I had queues of people and organizations wanting me to open their supermarkets, endorse their products or speak after dinner. I knew I wasn't going to starve. I was often told by some toffee-nosed players who thought it right to be offhand with the public that I talked too much, but the talent certainly paid off when I needed it. I also knew that I wasn't frightened of a camera, and Yorkshire Television had just started up in Leeds as I quit cricket. They signed me up for their sports programme (and I did a bit for their regional news and current affairs programmes just to show I could do more than just sport) and recently I've been anchor man for the highly popular network series, 'Indoor League', which covers just about every pub sport from darts and bar billiards to one-arm wrestling.

At the beginning I was game for anything and I found my name leaping out of the headlines again in 1969 when I went on the boards as a night club comedian. I had no ambitions in that direction really—I did it because I accepted a silly bet made when I was in a club in the North East listening to a pretty poor comedian. I asked the owner what he was paying the man and was amazed when he said £250 a week. So I said it was a damned good living for nothing because the stories he was telling were so old and badly delivered into the bargain. Then someone who overheard me said, 'Do you think you could do a week up there in front of a crowd like this?' I've always found challenges hard to refuse so I put a bold face on and said, 'Yes—piece of cake', and the bet was struck. I approached the Lipthorpe brothers who own the Fiesta clubs at Sheffield and Stockton and they were willing to let me do a week. They paid me a bit of brass, too, and I had a marvellous time. They thought of a great idea to present me to the audience—projecting a film of me bowling at the audience on a paper screen and at just the right moment I burst through leaving the screen in shreds. It shook 'em rigid the first night. I went down a treat because I can make up my own original jokes as well as tell them properly. I kept it up seven nights a week for nearly a month before I realized that, much though I enjoyed it, I had other more important things to do. To be truthful, I got fed up with it. I much prefer after-dinner speaking to Round Tables and Rotary Clubs, particularly if I'm helping to make money for children's charities.

Not all my business ventures went so smoothly as my stint as a comedian. When I was still a player I found out that going into partnership with others wasn't up to much. I tried a sports shop in Skipton under my name but opted out after a year or so, and I also had an interest in a garage which also didn't work out for me. But I nearly had a major disaster in later years. I'm not the first sportsman to get taken for a ride and I was asked to join one enterprise which turned out to be very doubtful. In fact, there was terrible trouble with threats of legal action, and since it happened at the same time as my divorce went through I was in a pretty bad state. I lost quite a lot of money too, and I really had to get my head down and work my way out of the mess. I forgot about big business after that and stayed independent. Brian Close had an even worse time in another business deal. On the other hand, he is one of the luckiest men alive, considering the number of serious car crashes he has been involved in.

On the personal level, however, my own luck changed just at the time when I most needed it. I met a red-haired girl at a cricket match in Harrogate, and all my resolve about never becoming deeply involved again melted completely. Veronica rescued me in a sense because she was able to give me the warmth and comfort of a family home which I missed very much. It was complicated at first because we were both still married, but eventually she became my wife. Fortunately, she was able to discover at first hand that the ridiculous stories which proliferate about me to this day were all damned lies. More than once in the early days when we were keeping our romance a secret Veronica listened to people talking about the amazing night out they had just had with Fred Trueman and recounting drunken exploits which would have put Don Juan to shame. But she had been with me for a quiet dinner the same night, just the two of us! Naturally, she couldn't say anything, although she badly wanted to expose them for the liars they were. Anyway, it certainly opened her eyes. I am still regularly confronted by strange women who come and say, 'You kept my husband out a bit late at the club the other night, didn't you!', and I have to ask them who the hell they are and then tell them I've never met their husbands.

I'm also approached frequently by men I scarcely know who are trying to use me as an alibi. One night I went to speak at a dinner near Skipton and a man came to me and said he wanted a night out with a bird that night and would it be all right if he told his wife he had been out with me until three or four in the morning. I told him he could bloody well please himself but if his wife said anything to me I would tell her the truth, because I'd had enough trouble of that kind to last a dozen lifetimes. I even referred to the request during my speech in the hope that word would get round that F. S. Trueman was not going to be used as a doormat any more. I get furious when person after person comes up to me and says, 'My, but you are a reformed character these days, aren't you, Fred?' It's a wonder I don't smash them in the teeth for their damned cheek, because I'm the same now as I've always been. I find it even harder to take than the stranger who sees me in a pub with a pint in my hand just after I've walked in and calls out, 'See you're still drinking a lot, Fred!' If members of the public think this is the way they ought to approach me they are wrong. All they have to do is say 'Hallo, Fred' and I'll be only too pleased to speak back politely.

Seven years after I had stopped playing for Yorkshire I was still hearing stories about what I was supposed to have just said and done on the cricket field. And as late as 1974 another ludicrous legend was born. I went to see the Indians at Worcester and met some of the players and the manager, Colonel Adi Kari, for a chat. Two weeks later there was a story going round the dressing rooms like a bush fire that Fred Trueman had greeted Colonel Kari with the words, 'How nice it is to see you've got your colour back!' I was also told recently that there was a certain well-known personality going round the after-dinner circuit telling a dozen stories about me, none of them funny. I remember hearing exactly the same stories myself twenty-five years ago, but they were being told about Harold Larwood.

At least I can take comfort from the fact that stories, old and new, won't sour my marriage with Veronica. I didn't really know what happiness was all about until I met her, and I'm taking great care to see that this marriage doesn't go the same way as the first one. I often wonder what deeds I might have done on the cricket field had Veronica and I met when we were kids. I rarely go anywhere without her and when I have finished a speaking engagement or a personal appearance I just have a couple of glasses of wine, make my excuses and drive back home even if it's a hundred miles away (which it frequently is). Recently I was asked to go to South Africa and I told the people arranging the deal that I wouldn't go without Veronica. They agreed. She organizes my life for me, keeps my diary and is marvellous at negotiating deals. And whenever I go to play cricket she's there watching me. I still play most Sundays in the summer for my own club team, the Saints, and appear in a lot of MCC matches against public schools. I also get a lot of invitations to play overseas in exhibition matches and I reckon I'm just as good today as a lot of much younger county players and a few internationals. It's a great pity the Rothman's Cavaliers team isn't still going because it afforded a marvellous chance for the old-time greats to show, in short bursts, just how good they used to be. I played for them a lot before and after I retired from Yorkshire and remember a fabulous tour of the West Indies. Cricket of this kind is tremendous fun and a great relief for players and spectators alike from the deadly serious Test matches.

And if it had not been for privately organized tours I would never have visited India, Pakistan and South

Africa and the cricket enthusiasts in these countries would have been deprived of ever having a chance of seeing me. At the other end of the scale I helped to introduce the game of cricket to the underprivileged people of the Americas, where they play some strange game with a bat which looks like an overgrown rolling pin. It happened after I got my 300th Test wicket and Yorkshire organized a trip to the United States and Canada which turned out to be one of the most enjoyable tours of them all. Everyone loved it, players and spectators alike, although we played on some of the most curious grounds known to man. We stirred up a lot of interest too, because when we arrived to play at a club in Toronto they had filled their notice board with cuttings of stories and photographs about me from American and Canadian newspapers.

I recall another happy trip to India in 1956 when players were invited to help celebrate their cricket association's silver jubilee. Some cricketers shy off from tours to India and Pakistan because of the risk of stomach infection—I believe Geoff Boycott is one of them. But I took the advice of a doctor friend of mine who had served in Burma during the war and for the first and only time in my life became a regular drinker of the hard stuff. He told me to avoid water and orange juice and drink only whisky and soda! It was the last thing I wanted to do but I followed his advice right through the tour. Several of the others were laid low, including Tom Graveney and Willie Watson, but I never had any trouble. Geoff Boycott seems to have more problems than anyone else on tours to hot countries because he appears to hate the sun. He always plays with his shirt sleeves down and his collar up and is rarely seen on the beaches.

147

I often wish I could get through to Geoff and help him with some of his problems. I know all the difficulties that can beset a world-class player from Yorkshire having to deal with the MCC, and I would love to see him knock hell out of the Australians with the bat again. Other stars aren't above coming to me for advice. In 1975 when Dennis Lillee was playing here he sought me out and said, 'Fred, I'm in trouble—can you help?' I already knew he was, and I agreed. He may be an Aussie and a natural enemy but he's also a fellow fast bowler and a leading member of our union. I told him it would take quarter of an hour to sort him out. He was setting off on his run-up too quickly and his left arm and left shoulder were dropping too early. The next day he went out and got everything right—against England, I'm afraid. One absolutely perfect delivery beat John Edrich all ends up and knocked his middle stump out of the ground. As he came back to his run-up Dennis put his thumb up to me, which led to nasty telegrams asking what the hell was I doing telling an Australian how to bowl! But Trevor Bailey said that it was a great pity that some of the prima donnas who play cricket for England didn't have the sense to come and ask me for advice. Let me exempt Chris Old, the Yorkshire and England fast bowler, from the list because he often does, and I'm proud to help him. He tells me he's getting much closer to the stumps in his delivery stride as a result of my advice.

I'm always ready to coach anybody from internationals to schoolboy cricketers—because I feel an obligation to do so. In spite of all my troubles, I know I owe the game of cricket a great deal and I'm willing to put something back. I only wish I had more chances because I reckon I know as much about the art of fast bowling as anyone in the world and it's a pity to let this knowledge lie idle.

I'm not asking to be put on committees working to further the game of cricket because I'm sure it wouldn't work. I'm not prepared to change my personality and I know from past experience that frank and out-spoken views may be part of normal life in Yorkshire, but they are not always appreciated in the South, where the administration of cricket will always be centred. Even today you will get more privileges as a player if you come straight into a county side from university and/or talk with a posh accent, and that issue alone would bring out the worst in me. Anyway, I'm far too busy keeping pace with my business commitments. I scarcely have time for my hobbies. When I was younger I became a very fair snooker player, largely because nearly every hotel in those days had a snooker table. Jimmy Binks, Ray Illingworth and Brian Close were all useful cuemen too, but now most of the snooker rooms we played in have been converted into extra bars or lounges, which I think is a great pity. But my main outside interest since boyhood has been in birds—the pursuit of ornithology, I hasten to add. That may come as a surprise to the people who have credited me with a score sheet rivalling Casanova's in the pursuit of the skirted variety.

The rural scene has always been my natural habitat and I have studied the habits of birds ever since I can remember. My home in the rolling hills near Skipton is magnificently situated for watching them. In the garden I can see pheasants, which visit my lawn most days, goldfinches, bullfinches, wrens, great spotted and green woodpeckers, tree creepers, nuthatches, tits of all kinds and occasionally a bunting. I've got some of these quite tame now, and a cock robin comes and taps on the window every morning for his breakfast. At night I've spotted several species of owl, including a screech owl, barn owl and brown owl. I also think there's a short-eared owl knocking about, and regularly I see a heron flapping sedately across the valley. I was thrilled to bits recently when I discovered a pair of dippers and two kingfishers, right in the middle of Skipton. It's surprising for two such timid breeds to inhabit a built-up area, but I actually saw the kingfisher dive into a small stream, catch a fish, bring it into a tree, whack it against a branch and then swallow it. I found later that they have been there about three years so they must be breeding.

At one time I was very keen on shooting and had regular invitations to join parties on the superb grouse moors of Yorkshire, but these days I prefer just to watch birds, not blow them out of the sky. I'd much rather spend my time that way than get involved in public life.

There have been one or two attempts to interest me in politics, including invitations to stand as Conservative candidate, but I've steered clear. It's too underhand a business for me. I have political views and so did my dad. He started out as a Liberal, I believe, but was a staunch Conservative all the time I knew him and used to say to me and the others, 'Don't you ever bloody vote for the Socialists!' In fact, I think only one of the Trueman family supports Labour even today.

One of the great satisfactions of my life was that my father lived to see my entire career. He never changed one bit as long as I knew him, refused to move out of the old family home in Maltby even when I offered to arrange for him and my mother to live in a modern bungalow, and kept working at the pit until he retired. I knew he was terribly proud of me, although he never showed it, and so were my former workmates at Maltby

Main. If ever I put away the wickets, they used to write my match figures on a board and put it in front of the cage so my father could see how I was doing the moment he came up from the coal face. He ended up training youngsters, but he hated mining from start to finish. He always said he would retire the day he was sixty-five and he did. It fell on a Thursday, and he came home and burnt all his pit clothes in the back yard.

My father remained a major influence in my life until he died. Many's the time I went back home to Maltby with problems and we would talk them out. He was a very sensible and knowledgeable person and there was nothing I wouldn't discuss with him. He worried for me when I was doing badly, and got angry for me when I was being wrongly accused or unfairly dropped. And his advice in the crisis time was generally: 'Bugger 'em, they'll want you before you'll want them, son.' He could also get angry with me if he thought I was being stupid, and I took several bollockings about my batting. It offended his cricketing principles to see me go in and swing the bat, take chances and throw my wicket away. I used to argue with him that I couldn't really be expected to bowl fast all day and then bat like an opener. He said I had a point, but he believed I could bat well and he advised me to get my head down and play properly because it would improve my chances for Test selection. He was right, of course.

During his retirement he did a bit of gardening and came regularly to watch me play. On the day I retired I went home to see him and said, 'That's it, Dad—I'm finished.' He was sitting in the same place where, twenty years earlier, I had given him my first Yorkshire cap and I could see he was deeply moved again. He thought for a bit, then looked at me and said, 'Well, I've been very fortunate. I was there to see you start playing cricket and I've lived to see you finish. I can die happy now. And I'll never watch Yorkshire play again.'

He never did. And he died two years later at the age of seventy-eight. Mother, bless her, is still going strong and still living in the same house, although I had another go at trying to move her when Dad died. She's in her seventies and very independent. There's still a Trueman working at Maltby Main—Arthur, my elder brother, who lives close to my mother. My other brothers and sisters—Phyllis, Flo, John, Dennis and Helen—are all fit and happy and we remain a closely knit family, visiting each other regularly, and every Christmas we all turn up, wives and all, at the old family home in Maltby. But there is one family mystery which has puzzled us all for nearly forty years. I had another sister called Stella, who married a man called Chester Taylor when I was about nine. I can still remember the wedding. Chester was a fitter working in safety equipment at Maltby Main and he and Stella went to live in a colliery house down at Stainton, where I was born. But shortly afterwards, and before they had any children, Stella became ill and died. I think it must have broken Chester's heart, because the day after the funeral he simply disappeared, never turning up at the cottage or the pit again. None of us has ever seen or heard of him from that day to this. If I remember him rightly, he was more or less an orphan and had no family so there was nowhere we could inquire. All through the years I've been playing cricket round the world—in a blaze of publicity—I have half expected him to turn up to see me. If he's still alive, and he will be around sixty now, he must know that F. S. Trueman is his brother-in-law. We would all like to know what became of him.

Chapter 12

Save English Cricket!

I only wish I was starting my career all over again right now, because with the state of the game today I think I would be twice as successful. Cricket has changed from a side-on to a chest-on game and most of the batsmen leap around like cats on hot bricks before the bowler has released the ball. As for bowlers, you can count on the fingers of one hand the number of side-on bowlers, and side-on is the only way you stand a chance of bowling an outswinger, the deadliest ball of the lot.

As late as 1975 I played in a game against Somerset and removed four batsmen very quickly by swinging the ball away from the bat. Someone came to me afterwards and said, 'Do you mind—we don't play that way today!' Some of the field placings these days make me cringe, but the worst deterioration is in the art of batting. Moving before the ball is delivered gives the bowler an enormous advantage. The idea is to make your play a fraction of a second after the ball is released—Len Hutton was a master at that. And you never saw people like Gary Sobers, Neil Harvey, Peter May, Denis Compton or Tom Graveney rushing about all round the crease like most of them do today. Nowadays those who keep still, like Geoffrey Boycott or Clive Lloyd, are exceptions—they don't move a muscle until precisely the right moment.

If I were bowling today I wouldn't have to bowl at the

leg stump to turn the batsman round, because he's already there. His first line of defence has gone. I would be able to bowl leg and middle, move the ball away and stand a chance of hitting the off stump as well as finding an edge. And considering England hasn't a fast bowler in the same class as Brian Statham, Les Jackson or myself I would be on my own, knocking wickets down like skittles.

Chris Old and Geoff Arnold are only medium fast, and I doubt whether Willis would have been considered for a Test place in my time. And the choice of Bob Woolmer as England's third seamer completely took me by surprise because I'm two yards quicker than him right now. You can find faster bowlers than him playing in the Yorkshire Council League. It makes me sad when I remember that England would call on third seamers of the quality of Trevor Bailey. That man was such a fighter that he should have been a Yorkshireman. Bowlers today seem to have forgotten how to attack. In 1975 I sat at the Oval commentating for the BBC and watched Derek Underwood bowling on a good wicket against Australia with a fine leg and another fielder behind square and fine as well. He should have been throwing the ball up in the air at the off stump or just outside and, with five in the cover, making them drive the ball. But he seemed incapable of doing it. He ended up with just over one wicket per Test match and played in all four! If I didn't get four or five wickets in each innings I didn't play in the next Test.

In fact, I'd say that the present England squad has only one player of true world stature and that's Alan Knott. He is the best wicket keeper in the world at the moment. In the whole of English cricket there is, in my view, only one batsman of true international standard and he won't play for his country. I've personally tried to find out the real reason behind Geoffrey Boycott's attitude, but without success. He says he wants to concentrate on improving the Yorkshire team, which is hard to quarrel with, but I feel he could still do that and return to the England side. I'm sure that he has designs on the England captaincy and much has been made of his alleged reluctance to play under Mike Denness, but he didn't seem to change his attitude when Tony Grieg took over. What is also very significant is that the only truly successful captains we've had since the last war were both Yorkshiremen—Len Hutton and Ray Illingworth. They won the Ashes back for England.

Trouble is England just hasn't got a man good enough for the job of captain of England, if you rule out Ray Illingworth and Brian Close, who are aged forty-four and forty-five respectively. In fact the present England side is the worst since the late forties when at least we had batsmen like Len Hutton, Cyril Washbrook, Gilbert Parkhouse, Jack Ikin, Godfrey Evans, Bill Edrich, Wally Hammond and Denis Compton—but no bowlers. The Aussies wiped the floor with us then, but there's hardly a man playing for England now who would have made that side. And I can't put the blame on the selectors, because I'm unable to suggest any alternatives. There just aren't any. God knows when we'll ever get the Ashes back, because the Aussies have got at least four world class players to pick—Greg Chappell, Rodney Marsh, Dennis Lillee and Jeff Thomson and plenty of others shaping up. As for the West Indies, even though they have only got two in the same bracket—Clive Lloyd and Andy Roberts—that's twice as many as us.

A lot of fuss has been made about David Steele, but I consider him just a good county man. The way he plays off the front foot means all you need to do is put your mid-off slightly deeper, bring your extra cover a little bit wider and pitch the ball up at off and middle. You may not get him out, if he's lucky, but he won't put any runs on the board, so it doesn't matter—you can put them out at the other end.

There is a long-term solution to this tragic situation—get every foreign player out of every county side. I've nothing against Clive Lloyd and company—they are lovely fellows—but out of the pool of 190 county cricketers only about a hundred can play for England. The only way this country will ever get a great team again is when we have seventeen county teams all playing eleven men all eligible to be picked for England. It's no use bringing out new rules to restrict foreign players to two per side because they will play middle order batsmen and that is precisely where England is weakest. All the heaviest scorers in the history of cricket, with the odd exception like Len Hutton, Herbert Sutcliffe or Jack Hobbs, are people like Don Bradman, Walter Hammond, Everton Weekes, Frank Worrell, Gary Sobers, Peter May, Denis Compton, Neil Harvey—the list is endless. They went in after the opening batsman had taken the edge off the bowling and after the shine had gone off the ball. Then they could get stuck in and make merry. There are players getting all the practice they need in the middle order in England county cricket who go back to play in their national side and knock hell out of ours. I'm not saying that every county should be as proud as Yorkshire and refuse to play anyone who wasn't born in the county, but there must be English kids with the right potential who just aren't getting the chance to which they are entitled.

Of course, Yorkshire are penalized heavily because

they won't change their tradition. Indeed they might be winning the championship now if they only had to play against other Englishmen at county level. The record speaks for itself—they beat Warwickshire out of sight in the County Championship because all their overseas stars were missing, hammered Hampshire at Sheffield when Roberts, Greenidge and Richards couldn't play, and they've beaten Surrey, Northamptonshire and Gloucestershire for exactly the same reason. It proves the point that English cricket is incredibly weak under the false surface of stars from overseas.

It would be an enormous step forward if a proper national coaching system could be set up and run by people who have proved themselves in the game, instead of leaving it in the hands of well-meaning amateurs like school teachers. I was lucky when I was a kid to have teachers who really tried to help me, but it wasn't until I came under an old professional like Cyril Turner that I began to find out what cricket was all about. I didn't even know how to hold the ball properly, never mind bowl it, until he showed me how. And yet when the administration had a chance not long ago to make real progress in the spotting and bringing on of young talent, they messed it up. They decided to appoint a national coach, and one or two great old players wanted the job. But who did they appoint? A school teacher! There must be kids with real potential all over the place, particularly in the Northern working-class areas where they learn from an early age that they'll have to fight for anything in his life, like I had to. I don't think it would be hard to find them if a little common sense was used and a proper system set up using the experience of international players who have now retired but are still fit—and there are plenty willing to pitch in. We will have to do it if we are to stop cringing whenever the England cricket team faces up to the West Indians or the Aussies.

Probably the most urgent problem facing the game is to set its administration right. A lot of the old guard who still secretly believe the game is really for amateurs and gentlemen from Oxbridge are clinging grimly on to the reins. They must be swept aside and embalmed in the Long Room at Lord's, then a start can be made on the long-term solutions.

And then the game should be commercialized properly. A start has been made, like the Commercial Union Test series in 1975 which proved that cricket is one of the greatest sporting commodities in the world when it is organized intelligently. It's a big step forward from my day, when the Rothman's Cavaliers team, a great idea to promote the talents of older players, withered and died because it didn't get the right encouragement. And the establishment considered that paying a few PRO pillocks a lot of money to tell players which cocktail party to attend was the best way to get support from big business. But the real commercialization of cricket is still in its infancy and bad mistakes are being made today. The Gillette Cup and the Benson & Hedges competitions are reasonable because they encourage proper cricket. The bowlers can use a proper run-up and there are sixty-odd overs. But I think the Sunday League should be scrapped. The bowlers are forced to use a limited run-up which means they can't get their proper pace. Spinners aren't being helped either, but the batsman is not handicapped and this leads to defensive field placings. These deadly defensive attitudes are spilling over into the three-day county game and our youngsters are being infected by the disease. The Sunday League is also placing a tremendous strain on men who often finish playing in Manchester or Leeds on a Saturday evening, pack their bags and drive through the night to Kent or Somerset, play all day Sunday, pack their bags again and come all the way back to start playing again on the Monday. We're breeding a race of automat cricketers and it shows on their faces. They look so bloody miserable out there on the field when really they are the luckiest people in the world. I know they sometimes have it hard but they should think about the millions of people who have to get up at half past six in the morning and stand at a factory bench or a conveyor belt all day. I know what it's like because I had a basinful before I managed to break into professional cricket. At least cricketers don't have to start until eleven in the morning and they are out in the fresh air all day. The game can be real fun if you set about it the right way.

If the quality of play is to be improved quickly, then county games should be extended to four days and wickets covered. Spin bowlers should be encouraged to throw the ball up in the air again, which will in turn encourage batsmen to play shots. Padding-up and pushing at short-pitched deliveries is a one-way ticket to boredom.

On second thoughts, perhaps I would rather not be starting my career again. At least I had the privilege of succeeding in what I consider was the golden era of cricket when every Test side was full of great players, with others just as good clamouring to get in, and when the whole nation frequently hung breathless on the result of a Test match. And every county championship was riveting enough to pack grounds round the country.

My career certainly wasn't all wine and roses, but by hell it was exciting. And the satisfaction I feel when I look back, re-live the records I broke and polish the trophies in my sideboard is trebled by the knowledge that I had to fight every inch of the way. I will never be accepted by the Establishment as long as I live, and I think I prefer it that way. No honour will come my way, I will never be knighted like Len Hutton (can you imagine it—Sir Freddie Trueman!) or wear a C.B.E. after my name like Brian Statham.

Harold Wilson, who has dished out a great many distinctions in his time, did give me a rather special, if unofficial, title once. He called me the greatest living Yorkshireman, for which I thank him.

But the men who bowed and scraped and stood to attention for their O.B.E.s, C.B.E.s and M.B.E.s are welcome to them. I have a letter written to me by the great Herbert Sutcliffe, a man who knew and batted against and with bowlers like Harold Larwood, Wilfred Rhodes, George Hirst and Hedley Verity, when I had taken my 250th Test wicket.

It said: 'I am amazed at the way you have always kept going despite bowling so fast. In figures alone, this must prove that you are the greatest bowler the world has ever seen.'

That'll do me!

24   Back to the nets at Derbyshire CCC after retirement, April 1972

25   The *Trueman*: a boat belonging to a company which named trawlers after cricketers whose names had seven letters. She lived up to her name, for she subsequently blew up in the North Sea

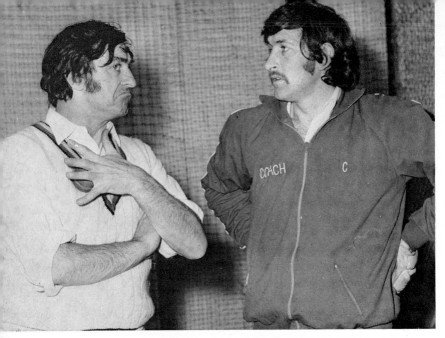

26   A load of . . .? With Chris Wilkins of Derbyshire, 1972

27   On a charity mission for paraplegics, New Zealand, April 1972

28 Introducing Yorkshire Television's 'The Indoor League', the programme which features pubs and clubs

29 With my second wife Veronica—the best thing that ever happened to me, 1973

30 With Mr Harold Wilson, who was declared Pipeman of the Decade in January 1976. I was Pipeman of the Year, 1975

THE NORTHERN CRICKET SOCIETY • 1969

Farewell, Freddie!

★

WICKETS: 2,302
(Average: 18.27)
TEST WKTS: 307
(Average: 21.54)
HAT-TRICKS : 4
5 W. in Inns: 126
10 W. in Mtch: 25
5 WICKETS IN A
TEST INNS.: 17
10 WKTS IN A
TEST MATCH: 3
BEST BOWLING (C):
8-28, Yorks v. Kent. '54
BEST BOWLING (T):
8-31. E. v. India, '52
100 W. IN SEASON:
~ 12 TIMES
NUMBER OF INNS:
~ 711.
TOTAL RUNS: 9,195
NOT OUTS : 120
CENTURIES: 3
(104, Y. v. Northants, '63.
100* E. XI v. Young E., '63
101, Yorks v. Middx, '65)
FIFTIES : 26
CATCHES: 438.

★

ROYMAN
BROWNE
'69

We shall miss you... so will Cricket!

Cover illustration of the Northern Cricket Society's annual maga-
zine for 1969 which, among other things, celebrated my retirement.

Fred Trueman's Cricketing Career Statistics

Prepared by Roy D. Wilkinson

ABBREVIATIONS

A., Aust.	Australia
Av	Average
b	Bowled
c	Caught (off Fred Trueman's bowling)
Ct	Caught (by Fred Trueman when fielding)
HS	Highest score
hw	Hit wicket
In	Innings
Ind.	India
lbw	Leg before wicket
M	Maiden
Mtch(s)	Match(es)
NO	Not out
N.Z.	New Zealand
O	Overs
R	Runs
ro	Run out
S.A.	South Africa
st	Stumped
W.I.	West Indies
W	Wicket(s)
†	8-ball overs
*	Not out

ALL FIRST-CLASS MATCHES—BOWLING AND FIELDING

Season	Mtchs	O	M	R	W	Av	5 W in In	10 W in Mtch	How wkts taken c	b	lbw	hw	Ct
1949	8	233.3	49	719	31	23.19	1	—	18	10	3	—	2
1950	14	290.1	43	876	31	28.25	—	—	19	9	3	—	5
1951	30	737.4	166	1852	90	20.57	6	1	43	39	8	—	21
1952	9	282.2	58	841	61	13.78	5	—	28	31	2	—	5
1953	15	447.1	77	1411	44	32.06	2	1	28	13	3	—	15
1953–54 (W.I.)	8	319.4	81	909	27	33.66	1	—	14	6	7	—	7
1954	33	808.2	188	2085	134	15.55	10	—	49	62	23	—	32
1955	31	996.4	214	2454	153	16.03	8	3	70	63	17	3	26
1956	31	588.4	133	1383	59	23.44	2	—	26	26	6	1	21
1956–57 (Ind.)	2	61	9	204	8	25.50	—	—	5	2	—	1	—
1957	32	842.2	184	2303	135	17.05	9	2	59	56	19	1	36
1958	30	638.5	176	1414	106	13.33	6	—	41	46	18	1	22
1958–59 (A. and N.Z.)	17	265.1† 100.2	61	1067	57	18.71	4	1	23	24	9	1	16
1959	30	1077.4	269	2730	140	19.50	6	—	59	63	18	—	24
1959–60 (W.I.)	10	342.3	86	883	37	23.86	2	—	12	17	8	—	11
1960	32	1068.4	275	2447	175	13.98	12	4	79	79	16	1	22
1960–61 (S.A.)	4	114.4	16	326	22	14.81	1	—	9	12	1	—	2
1961	34	1180.1	302	3000	155	19.35	11	4	80	62	10	3	13
1962	33	1141.5	273	2717	153	17.75	5	1	84	53	15	1	24
1962–63 (A. and N.Z.)	12	229.3† 121.2	54	1020	55	18.54	4	1	37	14	3	1	9

	M	O	M	R	W	Av	5 W in In	10 W in Mtch	c	b	lbw	hw	Ct
1963	27	844.3	207	1955	129	15.15	10	5	71	42	15	1	15
1963–64 (W.I.)	2	49	12	124	9	13.77	—	—	4	3	2	—	2
1964	31	833.1	171	2194	100	21.94	3	—	53	31	16	—	19
1964–65 (W.I.)	3	79.3	18	253	11	23.00	1	1	5	5	1	—	1
1965	30	754.4	180	1811	127	14.25	10	1	70	39	16	2	17
1966	33	859.1	203	2040	111	18.37	2	—	55	38	18	—	22
1967	31	595	135	1610	75	21.46	2	—	38	30	7	—	31
1967–68 (Ind.)	1	18	2	58	1	58.00	—	—	—	1	—	—	1
1968	29	515	116	1375	66	20.83	3	—	35	22	9	—	16
1969	1	21	1	93	2	46.50	—	—	1	1	—	—	1
Total	603	494.4† 15962.3	3759	42154	2304	18.29	126	25	1115	899	273	17	438

ALL FIRST-CLASS MATCHES FOR YORKSHIRE

Mtchs	O	M	R	W	Av	5 W in In	10 W in Mtch		How wkts taken				Ct
								c	b	lbw	hw		
459	12195.1	2906	29890	1745	17.12	97	20	830	698	206	11		324

COUNTY CHAMPIONSHIP MATCHES

Mtchs	O	M	R	W	Av	5 W in In	10 W in Mtch		How wkts taken				Ct
								c	b	lbw	hw		
381	10353.2	2463	25341	1488	17.03	83	17	716	585	178	9		278

For YORKSHIRE

    v Derbyshire 10 for 90 at Bradford, 1957
                 11 for 123 at Sheffield, 1961
    v Essex 11 for 94 at Southend, 1961
           10 for 67 at Bradford, 1966
    v Gloucestershire 11 for 101 at Huddersfield, 1955
                  10 for 65 at Bradford, 1963
    v Hampshire 12 for 62 at Portsmouth, 1960
    v Kent 10 for 136 at Scarborough, 1953
    v Leicestershire 12 for 58 at Sheffield, 1961
    v Northamptonshire 14 for 125 at Sheffield, 1960
    v Nottinghamshire 11 for 94 at Sheffield, 1951
                  10 for 94 at Scarborough, 1955
                  10 for 142 at Worksop, 1962
    v Surrey 14 for 123 at The Oval, 1960
    v Sussex 13 for 77 at Hove, 1965
    v Warwickshire 10 for 73 at Bradford, 1960
              10 for 36 at Birmingham, 1963
    v Cambridge Univ. 11 for 75 at Cambridge, 1957
    v Oxford Univ. 10 for 32 at Oxford, 1955
    v West Indies 10 for 81 at Middlesbrough, 1963

For ENGLAND

    v Australia 11 for 88 at Leeds, 1961
    v West Indies 11 for 152 at Lord's, 1963
             12 for 119 at Birmingham, 1963

For MCC

    v Otago 13 for 79 at Dunedin, 1958–59
    v Otago Invitation XI 11 for 83 at Dunedin, 1962–62

8 WICKETS IN AN INNINGS (10)

For YORKSHIRE

v Essex	8 for 37 at Bradford, 1966
v Gloucestershire	8 for 45 at Bradford, 1963
v Kent	8 for 28 at Dover, 1954
v Nottinghamshire	8 for 68 at Sheffield, 1951
	8 for 53 at Nottingham, 1951
	8 for 84 at Worksop, 1962
v Sussex	8 for 36 at Hove, 1965
v Minor Counties	8 for 70 at Lord's, 1949

For ENGLAND

v India	8 for 31 at Manchester, 1952

For MCC

v Otago	8 for 45 at Dunedin, 1958–59

HAT TRICKS (4)

For YORKSHIRE

v Nottinghamshire	at Nottingham, 1951
	at Scarborough, 1955
	at Bradford, 1963
v MCC	at Lord's, 1958

HOW HE TOOK HIS 2,304 WICKETS

Caught	1115	(48.4%)
Bowled	899	(39.1%)
lbw	273	(11.8%)
Hit wicket	17	(0.7%)
Total	2304	(100%)

ALL FIRST-CLASS MATCHES—BATTING

Season	Mtchs	In	NO	R	HS	Av	How out				
							c	b	lbw	st	ro
1949	8	6	2	12	10	3.00	2	2	—	—	—
1950	14	15	9	23	4*	3.83	3	2	—	1	—
1951	30	24	7	114	25	6.70	3	8	1	5	—
1952	9	4	3	40	23*	40.00	—	1	—	—	1
1953	15	16	2	131	34	9.35	—	10	1	2	—
1953–54 (W.I.)	8	9	3	81	20	13.50	2	3	1	—	—
1954	33	35	5	270	50*	9.00	10	18	—	—	2
1955	31	38	8	391	74	13.03	14	13	2	—	1
1956	31	30	3	358	58	13.25	9	15	1	2	—
1956–57 (Ind.)	2	4	2	96	46*	48.00	1	—	—	1	—
1957	32	41	14	405	63	15.00	8	12	2	3	2
1958	30	35	7	453	61	16.17	15	12	1	—	—
1958–59 (A. and N.Z.)	17	21	2	312	53	16.42	10	5	3	1	1
1959	30	40	9	602	54	19.41	14	10	4	2	—
1959–60 (W.I.)	10	13	2	153	37	13.90	6	3	2	—	—
1960	32	40	5	577	69	16.48	20	10	4	—	1
1960–61 (S.A.)	4	5	1	139	59	34.75	2	2	—	—	—
1961	34	48	6	809	80*	19.26	26	14	2	—	—
1962	33	42	4	840	63	22.10	20	10	7	1	—
1962–63 (A. and N.Z.)	12	14	—	194	38	13.85	11	3	—	—	—
1963	27	41	6	783	104	22.37	26	6	1	—	2

	Mtchs	In	NO	R	HS	Av	c	b	lbw	st	ro
1963–64 (W.I.)	2	2	—	28	28	14.00	—	1	—	1	—
1964	31	39	4	595	77	17.00	19	12	3	—	1
1964–65 (W.I.)	3	2	—	24	23	12.00	2	—	—	—	—
1965	30	39	2	636	101	17.18	14	16	7	—	—
1966	33	43	4	448	43	11.48	26	7	4	1	1
1967	31	33	5	342	34	12.21	19	6	3	—	—
1967–68 (Ind.)	1	2	—	42	33	21.00	—	1	—	1	—
1968	29	30	5	296	45	11.84	13	6	4	—	2
1969	1	2	—	37	26	18.50	1	—	—	1	—
Total	603	713	120	9231	—	15.56	296	208	53	22	14

ALL FIRST-CLASS MATCHES FOR YORKSHIRE

Mtchs	In	NO	R	HS	Av		How out			
						c	b	lbw	st	ro
459	533	81	6852	104	15.15	226	157	42	14	13

COUNTY CHAMPIONSHIP MATCHES

Mtchs	In	NO	R	HS	Av		How out			
						c	b	lbw	st	ro
381	448	65	5928	104	15.47	190	134	34	12	13

CENTURIES (3)

For YORKSHIRE

v Middlesex	101	at	Scarborough, 1965
v Northamptonshire	104	at	Northampton, 1963

For an ENGLAND XI

v Young England XI	100*	at	Scarborough, 1963

FIFTIES (26)

For YORKSHIRE

v Derbyshire	58	at	Sheffield, 1961
v Essex	54	at	Colchester, 1959
v Gloucestershire	50*	at	Bristol, 1954
	58	at	Sheffield, 1956
	61	at	Bristol, 1958
	77	at	Sheffield, 1964
v Hampshire	58*	at	Bradford, 1958
	53	at	Bournemouth, 1958
	51*	at	Bournemouth, 1961
	55	at	Middlesbrough, 1965
v Kent	69	at	Gravesend, 1960
v Lancashire	54*	at	Sheffield, 1961
v Leicestershire	74	at	Leicester, 1955
	52	at	Leeds, 1960
v Middlesex	54	at	Lord's, 1964
v Somerset	63	at	Leeds, 1957
v Surrey	50	at	Bradford, 1964
v Warwickshire	57	at	Harrogate, 1964
v Worcestershire	56	at	Harrogate, 1960
v New Zealand	60	at	Bradford, 1965
v West Indies	55	at	Middlesbrough, 1963

For T. N. PEARCE'S XI

v Australia	80*	at	Scarborough, 1961
v West Indies	50	at	Scarborough, 1963

For PLAYERS

v Gentlemen	63	at	Lord's, 1962

For MCC

v Combined XI	53	at	Perth, 1958–59

For COMMONWEALTH XI

v Transvaal	59	at	Johannesburg, 1960–61

CENTURY PARTNERSHIPS (7)

For YORKSHIRE

v Leicestershire	133 for the 8th wkt with R. Illingworth at Leicester, 1955 (FT 74; RI 61)
	102 for the 6th wkt with K. Taylor at Sheffield, 1961 (FT 43; KT 159)
v Middlesex	147 for the 8th wkt with J. P. G. Chadwick at Scarborough, 1965 (FT 101; JC 59)
v Northamptonshire	166 for the 6th wkt with D. B. Close at Northampton, 1963 (FT 104; DBC 161)
v Somerset	116 for the 8th wkt with R. Illingworth at Leeds, 1957 (FT 63; RI 97)
v Cambridge Univ.	114 for the 6th wkt with D. B. Close at Cambridge, 1963 (FT 49; DBC 86)

For an ENGLAND XI

v Young England XI	120* for the 8th wkt with T. E. Bailey at Scarborough, 1963 (FT 100*; TEB 44*)

MOST RUNS OFF ONE 6-BALL OVER

26 (440666) off D. Shackleton, Yorkshire v Hampshire, Middlesbrough, 1965. (Subsequently, in the second innings, Yorkshire were all out for 23, which is their lowest total in any first-class match.)

HOW HIS 593 COMPLETED INNINGS ENDED

Caught	296	(49.9%)
Bowled	208	(35.1%)
lbw	53	(8.9%)
Stumped	22	(3.7%)
Run out	14	(2.4%)
Total	593	(100.0%)

TEST MATCHES—BOWLING AND FIELDING

Season	Mtchs	O	M	R	W	Av	5 W in In	10 W in Mtch	Ct
1952 (Ind.)	4	119.4	25	386	29	13.31	2	—	1
1953 (Aust.)	1	26.3	4	90	4	22.50	—	—	2
1953–54 (W.I.)	3	133.2	27	420	9	46.66	—	—	—
1955 (S.A.)	1	35	4	112	2	56.00	—	—	—
1956 (Aust.)	2	75	13	184	9	20.44	1	—	4
1957 (W.I.)	5	173.3	34	455	22	20.68	1	—	7
1958 (N.Z.)	5	131.5	44	256	15	17.06	1	—	6
1958–59 (Aust.)	3	87†	11	276	9	30.66	—	—	3
1958–59 (N.Z.)	2	44.5	17	105	5	21.00	—	—	4
1959 (Ind.)	5	177.4	53	401	24	16.70	—	—	5
1959–60 (W.I.)	5	220.3	62	549	21	26.14	1	—	6
1960 (S.A.)	5	180.3	31	508	25	20.32	1	—	4
1961 (Aust.)	4	164.4	21	529	20	26.45	2	1	2
1962 (Pak.)	4	164.5	37	439	22	19.95	1	—	6
1962–63 (Aust.)	5	158.3†	9	521	20	26.05	1	—	7
1962–63 (N.Z.)	2	88	29	164	14	11.71	1	—	—
1963 (W.I.)	5	236.4	53	594	34	17.47	4	2	3
1964 (Aust.)	4	133.3	25	399	17	23.47	1	—	3
1965 (N.Z.)	2	96.3	23	237	6	39.50	—	—	1
Total	67	245.3† 2202.3	522	6625	307	21.57	17	3	64

10 WICKETS IN A TEST MATCH (3)

v Australia	11 for 88 (5 for 58, 6 for 30) at Leeds, 1961
v West Indies	12 for 119 (5 for 75, 7 for 44) at Birmingham, 1963
	11 for 152 (6 for 100, 5 for 52) at Lord's, 1963

7 WICKETS IN A TEST INNINGS (3)

	O	M	R	W
v India, Manchester 1952	8.4	2	31	8
v West Indies, Birmingham, 1963	14.3	2	44	7
v New Zealand, Christchurch, 1962–63	30.2	9	75	7

HOW HE TOOK HIS TEST WICKETS

Caught	161	(52.4%)
Bowled	104	(33.9%)
lbw	39	(12.7%)
Hit wicket	3	(1.0%)
Total	307	(100.0%)

TEST MATCH BOWLING AGAINST EACH COUNTRY

For ENGLAND	Mtchs	O	M	R	W	Av	5 W in In	10 W in Mtch	Ct
		245.3†							
v Australia	19	399.4	83	1999	79	25.30	5	1	21
v India	9	297.2	78	787	53	14.84	2	—	6
v New Zealand	11	361.1	113	762	40	19.05	2	—	11
v Pakistan	4	164.5	37	439	22	19.95	1	—	6
v South Africa	6	215.3	35	620	27	22.96	1	—	4
v West Indies	18	764	176	2018	86	23.46	6	2	16
		245.3†							
Total	67	2202.3	522	6625	307	21.57	17	3	64

TEST MATCH BOWLING IN ENGLAND

For ENGLAND	Mtchs	O	M	R	W	Av	5 W in In	10 W in Mtch	Ct
v Australia	11	399.4	63	1202	50	24.04	4	1	11
v India	9	297.2	78	787	53	14.84	2	—	6
v New Zealand	7	228.2	67	493	21	23.47	1	—	7
v Pakistan	4	164.5	37	439	22	19.95	1	—	6
v South Africa	6	215.3	35	620	27	22.96	1	—	4
v West Indies	10	410.1	87	1049	56	18.73	5	2	10
Total	47	1715.5	367	4590	229	20.04	14	3	44

TEST MATCH BOWLING OVERSEAS

For ENGLAND	Mtchs	O	M	R	W	Av	5 W in In	10 W in Mtch	Ct
v Australia	8	245.3†	20	797	29	27.48	1	—	10
v New Zealand	4	132.5	46	269	19	14.15	1	—	4
v West Indies	8	353.5	89	969	30	32.30	1	—	6
		245.3†							
Total	20	486.4	155	2035	78	26.08	3	—	20

TEST MATCHES—BATTING

Season	Mtchs	In	NO	R	HS	Av
1952 (Ind.)	4	2	1	17	17	17.00
1953 (Aust.)	1	1	—	10	10	10.00
1953–54 (W.I.)	3	4	1	38	19	12.66
1955 (S.A.)	1	2	2	8	6*	—
1956 (Aust.)	2	3	—	9	7	3.00
1957 (W.I.)	5	4	3	89	36*	89.00
1958 (N.Z.)	5	4	1	52	39*	17.33
1958–59 (Aust.)	3	6	—	75	36	12.50
1958–59 (N.Z.)	2	2	1	42	21*	42.00
1959 (Ind.)	5	6	—	61	28	10.16
1959–60 (W.I.)	5	8	2	86	37	14.33
1960 (S.A.)	5	8	1	99	25	14.14
1961 (Aust.)	4	6	—	60	25	10.00
1962 (Pak.)	4	2	—	49	29	24.50
1962–63 (Aust.)	5	7	—	142	38	20.28
1962–63 (N.Z.)	2	2	—	14	11	7.00
1963 (W.I.)	5	10	1	82	29*	9.11
1964 (Aust.)	4	6	1	42	12*	8.40
1965 (N.Z.)	2	2	—	6	3	3.00
Total	67	85	14	981	—	13.81

Highest score: 39* v New Zealand at The Oval, 1958, in 25 minutes, and including 3 sixes off A. M. Moir

TEST MATCH BATTING AGAINST EACH COUNTRY

For ENGLAND	Mtchs	In	NO	R	HS	Av
v Australia	19	29	1	338	38	12.07
v India	9	8	1	78	28	11.14
v New Zealand	11	10	2	114	39*	14.25
v Pakistan	4	2	—	49	29	24.50
v South Africa	6	10	3	107	25	15.28
v West Indies	18	26	7	295	37	15.52
Total	67	85	14	981	—	13.81

COUNTY CHAMPIONSHIP MATCHES— BOWLING AND FIELDING

For YORKSHIRE	Mtchs	O	M	R	W	Av	5 W in In	10 W in Mtch	Ct
v Derbyshire	24	755.2	178	1850	108	17.12	7	2	17
v Essex	20	591.4	120	1492	96	15.54	7	2	9
v Glamorgan	17	371.1	100	858	54	15.88	4	—	13
v Glou'shire	23	528	122	1331	91	14.62	5	2	22
v Hampshire	22	603.5	174	1331	91	14.62	6	1	20
v Kent	20	491.1	92	1265	82	15.42	3	1	10
v Lancs	35	977.5	226	2307	128	18.02	8	—	18
v Leic'shire	22	593.2	131	1536	88	17.45	6	1	18
v Middlesex	28	754.5	159	2037	89	22.88	2	—	20
v North'shire	18	548.3	133	1372	65	21.10	4	1	22
v Nott'shire	29	786.4	190	1826	131	13.93	10	3	22
v Somerset	25	676.4	165	1572	108	14.55	3	—	22
v Surrey	32	910	222	2272	107	21.23	5	1	28
v Sussex	21	602.4	146	1557	79	19.70	4	1	12
v War'shire	24	654.1	183	1542	109	14.14	7	2	11
v Worc'shire	21	507.3	122	1193	62	19.24	2	—	14
Total	381	10353.2	2463	25341	1488	17.03	83	17	278

HOW HE TOOK HIS COUNTY CHAMPIONSHIP WICKETS

Caught	716	(48.1%)
Bowled	585	(39.3%)
lbw	178	(12.0%)
Hit wicket	9	(0.6%)
Total	1488	(100.0%)

COUNTY CHAMPIONSHIP MATCHES—BATTING

For YORKSHIRE	Mtchs	In	NO	R	HS	Av
v Derbyshire	24	27	4	338	58	14.69
v Essex	20	21	4	288	54	16.94
v Glamorgan	17	20	—	180	37	9.00
v Glou'shire	23	29	3	488	77	18.76
v Hampshire	22	31	5	573	58*	22.03
v Kent	20	21	—	264	69	12.57
v Lancs.	35	38	11	400	54*	14.81
v Leic'shire	22	25	2	417	74	18.13
v Middlesex	28	35	2	555	101	16.81
v North'shire	18	23	3	396	104	19.80
v Nott'shire	29	26	7	266	34*	14.00
v Somerset	25	27	3	372	63	15.50
v Surrey	32	44	3	434	50	10.58
v Sussex	21	26	5	362	43	17.23
v War'shire	24	29	6	266	57	11.56
v Worc'shire	21	26	7	329	56	17.31
Total	381	448	65	5928	—	15.47

HOW HIS COUNTY CHAMPIONSHIP INNINGS ENDED

Caught	190	(49.6%)
Bowled	134	(35.0%)
lbw	34	(8.9%)
Stumped	12	(3.1%)
Run out	13	(3.4%)
Total	383	(100.0%)

GROUNDS

MATCHES PLAYED ON YORKSHIRE GROUNDS

	Mtchs	In	NO	R	HS	Av	O	M	R	W	Av	5 W in In	10 W in Mtch	Ct
Bradford	58	70	11	890	60	15.08	1376.4	324	3367	213	15.80	12	4	53
Harrogate	12	11	1	248	57	24.80	295.1	94	619	44	14.06	3	—	8
Huddersfield	5	6	2	25	12	6.25	162.2	33	432	32	13.50	2	1	4
Hull	20	23	2	182	39	8.66	550.2	129	1280	80	16.00	2	—	10
Leeds	48	57	11	679	63	14.76	1324.1	311	3368	181	18.60	8	1	46
Middlesbrough	12	16	1	325	55	21.66	303.3	74	696	54	12.88	4	1	10
Scarborough	61	77	22	1142	101	20.76	1425.4	267	4097	203	20.18	9	2	43
Sheffield	53	53	8	806	77	17.91	1560.3	356	3954	225	17.57	17	4	45
Total	269	313	58	4297	—	16.85	6998.2	1588	17813	1032	17.26	57	13	219

OTHER GROUNDS IN ENGLAND WHERE HE APPEARED IN 6 OR MORE MATCHES

	Mtchs	In	NO	R	HS	Av	O	M	R	W	Av	5 W in In	10 W in Mtch	Ct
Birmingham	18	20	5	161	29*	10.73	568.4	126	1580	79	20.00	6	2	9
Bournemouth	6	11	2	222	53	24.66	136.4	37	331	16	20.68	1	—	6
Bristol	9	10	2	143	61	17.87	180.4	37	479	28	17.10	—	—	5
Cambridge	12	11	2	167	49	18.55	283.2	87	629	45	13.97	2	1	7
Chesterfield	9	10	1	92	48	10.22	281.5	62	682	28	24.35	—	—	4
Hove	10	12	3	113	34	12.55	337.2	86	850	46	18.47	4	1	2
Leicester	12	15	2	223	74	17.15	304.2	61	770	36	21.38	2	—	10
Lord's	50	62	9	737	63	13.90	1488.2	324	4108	191	21.50	9	1	24
Manchester	25	32	9	286	40*	12.43	741	161	1854	83	22.33	3	—	15
Northampton	8	10	2	255	104	31.87	249.2	58	637	23	27.69	1	—	8
Nottingham	16	13	2	116	31	10.54	518.2	127	1232	77	16.00	5	—	14
Oxford	9	6	1	56	23	11.20	263.5	91	482	50	9.64	3	1	4
Taunton	8	8	1	114	42	16.28	208	55	453	28	16.17	—	—	4
The Oval	28	38	2	367	45	10.19	777.2	186	1851	103	17.97	6	1	28
Worcester	9	13	3	144	43	14.40	254	59	606	25	24.24	—	—	2

	Mtchs	In	NO	R	HS	Av	O	M	R	W	Av	5 W in In	10 W in Mtch	Ct
In Yorkshire	269	313	58	4297	101	16.85	6998.2	1588	17813	1032	17.26	57	13	219
Other grounds in England	275	328	52	3865	104	14.00	7758.1	1832	19497	1045	18.65	56	10	170
All grounds in England	544	641	110	8162	104	15.37	14756.3	3420	37310	2077	17.96	113	23	389
In Australia	21	27	1	445	53	17.11	494.4†	49	1596	67	23.82	3	—	19
In India	3	6	2	138	46*	34.50	79	11	262	9	29.11	—	1	1
In New Zealand	8	8	1	61	21*	8.71	221.4	66	491	45	10.91	5	2	6
In South Africa	4	5	1	139	59	34.75	114.4	16	326	22	14.81	1	—	2
In West Indies	23	26	5	286	37	13.61	790.4	197	2169	84	25.82	4	—	21
Total	603	713	120	9231	—	15.56	15962.3 / 494.4†	3759	42154	2304	18.29	126	25	438

Ball of Fire

CAREER STATISTICS AS CAPTAIN

	Mtchs	Won	Lost	Drawn
1962	2	1	—	1
1965	3	2	—	1
1966	2	1	1	—
1967	16	9	2	5
1968	7	4	1	2
1969	1	1	—	—
Total	31	18 (58.1%)	4 (12.9%)	9 (29%)

ONE-DAY CRICKET

GILLETTE CUP (FOR YORKSHIRE, 1963–68)

Mtchs	In	NO	R	HS	Av	O	M	R	W	Av	Ct
11	9	1	127	28	15.87	119.2	15	348	21	16.56	5

His best Gillette Cup performance was against Somerset at Taunton in 1965—10.2 overs, 4 maidens, 15 runs, 6 wickets—and this earned him the 'Man of the Match' award

JOHN PLAYER LEAGUE (FOR DERBYSHIRE, 1972)

Mtchs	In	NO	R	HS	Av	O	M	R	W	Av	Ct
6	4	1	28	10*	9.33	45	3	159	7	22.71	—

Index

Index

Index